THE PENGUIN CLASSICS

FOUNDER EDITOR (1944–64): E. V. RIEU

Editor: Betty Radice

CORNELIUS TACITUS was born about A.D. 56 and probably survived the emperor Trajan who died in 117. In a Rome keenly appreciative of elegance in the spoken and written word he gained distinction as an impressive orator, and one of his three surviving monographs, the *Dialogue*, is a historical survey of changes in oratorical style. His political career as a senator began under Vespasian (69–79) and developed under Titus (79–81) and Domitian (81–96). Despite the alleged reign of terror at the end of this period, he survived to enjoy the consulship in 97 and, fifteen years later, the highest civilian provincial governorship, that of Western Anatolia. His other monographs, the biographical *Agricola* and the ethnographical *Germania*, appeared within a short time of each other in 98. Of his later and major works, the *Histories* were intended to cover the years from Nero's death in 68 to that of Domitian in 96, and the *Annals* those from A.D. 14 to 68. Both books have survived, though mutilated. Tacitus was a friend of Pliny the Younger, who greatly admired him. He was married to the daughter of Julius Agricola, governor of Britain in the seventies and eighties. But the historian is generally reticent about himself, and we do not even know his place of origin, though Italy and southern France are possible candidates for this honour.

HAROLD MATTINGLY was born in 1884 and died in 1964. A distinguished numismatist, he is best known for his study of Roman coinage at the British Museum where he worked from 1910 to 1948. As a classical scholar and historian his interests were wide-ranging. He wrote over four hundred articles and books and his *Roman Imperial Civilization*, first published when he was seventy-two, embodied the reflections of a lifetime devoted to the study of the Roman world.

S. A. HANDFORD was born at Manchester in 1898 and educated at Bradford Grammar School and at Balliol College, Oxford, where he took a 'double first' in classics. He has been a lecturer in Swansea, and Lecturer and Reader at King's College, London. He has published several books on classical subjects, and has translated Caesar's *The Conquest of Gaul*, Sallust's *The Jugurthine War* and *The Conspiracy of Cataline* (in one volume) and Aesop's *Fables* for the Penguin Classics, besides revising the present volume.

TACITUS

THE AGRICOLA
AND THE
GERMANIA

TRANSLATED
WITH AN INTRODUCTION
BY H. MATTINGLY

TRANSLATION REVISED
BY S. A. HANDFORD

PENGUIN BOOKS

Penguin Books Ltd, Harmondsworth, Middlesex, England
Penguin Books, 625 Madison Avenue, New York, New York 10022, U.S.A.
Penguin Books Australia Ltd, Ringwood, Victoria, Australia
Penguin Books Canada Ltd, 2801 John Street, Markham, Ontario, Canada L3R 1B4
Penguin Books (N.Z.) Ltd, 182–190 Wairau Road, Auckland 10, New Zealand

—

This translation first published 1948
Reprinted 1951, 1954, 1960, 1962, 1964, 1965, 1967
Revised translation published 1970
Reprinted 1971, 1973, 1975, 1976, 1977, 1979, 1980

—

Made and printed in Great Britain by
Hazell Watson & Viney Ltd,
Aylesbury, Bucks
Set in Monotype Bembo

CONTENTS

The maps on pages 50 and 100 are reproduced by the courtesy of the Clarendon Press from H. Furneaux's edition of *Agricola* (revised by J. G. C. Anderson) and J. G. C. Anderson's edition of *Germania* respectively

PREFACE

It is now twenty-two years since the translation of Tacitus's *Agricola and Germania* (under the title *On Britain and Germany*) by Harold Mattingly first appeared. When this translation first appeared it was accepted as one of the best translations available of these two books; but in the course of time certain opinions have been revised, both about translations in general and about the approach to Tacitus's work. For these reasons, S. A. Handford and Penguins have produced this revision, taking the opportunity to correct a few inaccuracies. They wish to acknowledge their indebtedness, and that of all classical scholars, to Harold Mattingly, upon the foundation of whose original translation this text has been prepared. Harold Mattingly's original Introduction has been preserved substantially as he wrote it.

INTRODUCTION

THE *Agricola* of Tacitus, the biography of the most
famous governor of Roman Britain, is part of our
national story, and as such has a direct claim on our interest. The *Germania*, a detailed account of a great people that
had already begun to be a European problem in the first
century of our era, should still have a message for us in the
twentieth. The story of the hero and the story of strange
countries that were combined in Homer's *Odyssey* have
now, at a later stage of literature, come to receive separate
treatment.

The general reader may like to know that sections
XI–XIV of this Introduction are less immediately necessary to the understanding of the text than sections I–X,
and that the bibliography and some of the notes are
intended chiefly for classical students.

I. *Tacitus*

Cornelius Tacitus was born, probably in a country town
of *Gallia Narbonensis*, in A.D. 56 or 57 and died at some
time after 115. The son of a Roman Knight, he himself
rose to senatorial rank and passed through a normal
senatorial career. He was consul in 97 and governor of
Asia in 112–113. He was an intimate friend of Pliny the
Younger. Both were successful orators and distinguished
men of letters. Pliny was proud to be regarded as a pupil
of Tacitus and to be bracketed with him in popular

repute. He addressed to him a number of his published letters – two of them giving a detailed account of the eruption of Vesuvius for the use of Tacitus in his *Histories*. Of the private life of Tacitus we know very little indeed. He married the daughter of Agricola in 77, but he never mentions her name.

The first literary works of Tacitus, the *Agricola* and the *Germania*, were completed in A.D. 98. The *Dialogus de Oratoribus* is of uncertain date. Then came the major historical works – the *Histories*, covering the years 69–96, and the *Annals* (completed between 115 and 120), which started from the death of Augustus in 14 and continued to the death of Nero in 68. Both works have come down to us incomplete. Tacitus tells us that he had reserved for his old age an account of the happier age that followed the death of Domitian in 96. But it was never written. Did death overtake him, or had he lost the zest to write?

Tacitus was one of those Italians of sound old stock who brought to the service of the Empire a loyalty and devotion that recall the best days of the Republic. It was the destiny of Rome to rule the world, the destiny of the high-born Roman to share in that great task; and Rome now meant not the city only, but Italy as well. We may think of Tacitus as something like an officer of a colonial army and a colonial administrator rolled into one. He has a passionate belief in the 'career' as the thing that chiefly matters in life.

Men like Tacitus continued to pursue that career under emperors good or bad. He had experience of tyrants like

Nero and Domitian and of constitutional emperors like Vespasian, Nerva, and Trajan. He reflected much on his experience, and ended with the sad conclusion that one must not expect too much. Autocracy and freedom could not finally be reconciled. The fact was that imperial tyranny pressed hardest on the senators. The tyrant Domitian had forced the Senate to co-operate in his tyranny, and such men as Tacitus, constrained to vote against their consciences in condemnation of their own friends, burst out into violent denunciations as soon as the tyrant was safely dead. This was natural enough, but it leads Tacitus to judge the Empire somewhat unfairly. After all, it did confer on the world the great blessings of peace and order, and to Tacitus and men like him it opened up all that made their lives worth living.

As a historian Tacitus has several obvious defects. He is often amazingly careless about geography and military history. He is not deeply interested in the man in the street. He is not always just, as, for example, when he hints, on very slight grounds, that Domitian poisoned Agricola. He permits himself an occasional sneer at the enemies of Rome, more suitable to cheap journalism of any age than to a serious work of history. He mocks the Britons for adopting Roman civilization – poor, deluded slaves. He gibes at the Bructeri, butchering and butchered to provide a Roman holiday. He finds it 'glorious' that Roman legions should stand safely in reserve while their brave auxiliaries bear the brunt of battle. But he has great qualities. He has a lively imagination and a quick wit, he is manly and high-minded, and he is capable of genuine moral indignation, even if he occasionally directs it against rather trivial objects. There is enough in common between his age and ours for us to sympathize with his problems. The Roman Empire is, in fact, nearer to us spiritually than our own country in the Middle Ages.

The style of Tacitus grew under the influence of earlier writers such as Cicero and Sallust, but developed finally into something distinct and unique, like his own Germans.

Tacitus is fond of short sentences and shuns the long period. He is terse, fond of variety, given to inversion and poetic forms of expression. His works were probably all designed to be declaimed, in the first place. That is why a chapter so often ends with an epigram; it is a signal for applause before the next chapter begins. Many of these epigrams leave their sting behind them. But occasionally the form is there without the spirit, because what Tacitus actually has to say is quite simple and not really epigrammatic.

Tacitus's prose is exceptionally hard to render into another language. He was a great stylist – perhaps the greatest of the Roman Empire – and no translation can be really faithful to the original unless it reproduces at least something of his sombre magnificence and mordant wit.

II. *Agricola, the Man*

The name of Cn. Julius Agricola, the father-in-law of
Tacitus, is preserved on a lead pipe discovered on the
site of the legionary fortress at Chester; and a few letters
which certainly formed part of his name appear on one of
the surviving fragments of an inscription found in the
forum of Verulamium. But Tacitus judged rightly that it
was his own story that would confer immortality on
Agricola's memory.

To the details of his career recorded by Tacitus there is
little to add. He was born in A.D. 40. The 'Julius' in his
name and in that of his father suggests a possibility that an
ancestor may have been enfranchised by Julius Caesar.
The father wrote on the cultivation of the vine, and that
possibly led to his son's being named 'Agricola' (farmer).
The dates of Agricola's appointments were:

> Tribunus Militum in Britain, *c.* A.D. 61.
>
> Quaestor in Asia, 64.
>
> Tribunus Plebis in Rome, 66.
>
> Praetor in Rome, 68.
>
> Legatus Legionis XX in Britain, 70–73/4.
>
> Legatus Praetorius in Aquitania, 74–77.
>
> Consul in Rome for some months, 77 or 78.
>
> Legatus Praetorius in Britain, 78–84.
>
> Retirement in Rome, 84–93, and death in the
> latter year.

Agricola, then, during his long and honourable career
of public service, had the opportunity of acquiring an

unrivalled knowledge of the province of Britain. He had a good eye for the site of a fort and was an able tactician. But his strategy has been criticized and his seven years of campaigning did not produce very decisive or permanent results. His optimistic opinion that Ireland could be conquered and held by a single legion and a small force of auxiliaries (Chapter 24) might well make a thoughtful reader gasp. Tacitus's description of his father-in-law (in Chapter 35) as 'always an optimist and resolute in the face of difficulties' is perhaps a little truer than he intended; and we cannot refuse some sympathy to the 'cowards' who pleaded for a 'strategic retreat' because they thought that Agricola was asking for trouble by his bold dash into Caledonia (Chapter 25). Domitian can hardly be blamed for recalling him. Agricola had had a long innings, and troops were urgently needed at more vital spots on the Rhine and Danube. Tacitus awards very high praise to the civil government of Agricola both in Aquitania (Chapter 9) and in Britain (Chapter 19). In Britain too much was, perhaps, sacrificed to campaigning; for Agricola, as Tacitus admits, was in love with military glory (Chapter 5).

Agricola, like Tacitus, accepted the world as he found it. A good man himself, he was pained by Domitian's bad government. But he was sensible and would not sacrifice his life in a useless defiance of authority. The refusal of Domitian to make any use of Agricola's services after his return from Britain was very likely prompted by jealousy and fear. But there was no real evidence that he poisoned him, and Tacitus might have acknowledged this more frankly.

Of Agricola's personality each reader must judge for himself. Tacitus certainly loved and honoured him, and convinces us that he had good reason for so doing. But there are few intimate, or even personal, touches. We are never told any anecdote of his life in camp or town, of how he dealt with such and such a troublesome centurion or won over such and such a Scottish chief. We meet rebel Britons, Roman soldiers, Caledonian champions of freedom. But we hardly see them except as masses. One wonders whether Agricola himself did. The portrait of Agricola, then, has power both to attract and to impress, but it is rather the portrait of a career than of a man.

III. *Agricola, the Book*

The *Agricola* belongs to the class 'biography' and – to some extent – to the sub-class 'eulogy'. It is also a tribute to piety, for the object of the eulogy was Tacitus's own loved and honoured father-in-law. Such tributes to greatness were paid throughout classical antiquity. We need only mention the works of Xenophon, Isocrates, and Plutarch among the Greeks, and Cornelius Nepos and Suetonius among the Romans. There were two other Latin works – the *Bellum Iugurthinum* and *Catilina* of Sallust – which contributed much to the plan of the *Agricola*, even though neither of them is exactly a biography. Apart from Roman literary works, there were also the funeral orations customarily delivered over the illustrious dead.

The *Agricola* follows the common plan. In Chapters 1–3 the subject is introduced and explained; in Chapters 4–9 the life and career of Agricola are sketched down to his entry on the governorship of Britain. Then follows a digression – a description of Britain (Chapters 10–12) and a short history of the early conquest (Chapters 13–17). In Chapter 18 we come back to Agricola and follow his glorious career in Britain down to Chapter 38. The concluding Chapters, 39–46, describe his recall to Rome, his perils in retirement, and his death – ending with the thought of his undying fame.

The *Agricola* was probably written in A.D. 97–98, begun before the death of Nerva and completed afterwards. Tacitus was already planning to write a general history of the years 69–96, and the account of Britain in the *Agricola* has been regarded as a preparative study. But it is the biographical interest that is always to the fore. The reason why the main part of the work consists of historical narrative is simply that Agricola's title to fame was the fact that he played an important part in conquering Britain and thus extending the Roman frontier nearer to the extreme north of the known world.

But was the *Agricola* something more than a biography? Was it a tract in defence of political moderation? There is some truth in the suggestion, but it must not be overestimated. Agricola had certainly never opposed the tyrannical Domitian. He was a great man as far as he was allowed to be, but he knew when he must submit. For Agricola the defence may be accepted as adequate; but the charge of subservience could equally well be levelled at Tacitus and his friends, and here the defence is less successful. They had suffered in silence, acquiescing against their consciences in the condemnation of their friends. They believed in the importance of their careers and felt no call to fruitless martyrdom. But they were trying to make the best of both worlds – to survive under a bad emperor and to resume full rank as patriots under a good one. Tacitus's own conscience is a little uneasy. In Chapter 2 there is shame as well as sorrow in the story of Domitian's war on culture and merit; and in Chapter 45 – the description of Domitian's final reign of terror – there is almost a confession of guilt – 'we senators watched in shame'. Those who fell victims to Domitian were not all desperate men rushing to their doom; they included *promptissimus quisque*, all the 'live wires', one might almost say. There is, therefore, an element of apology for the life of Tacitus and his friends; but it is only a subordinate part of the book.

The *Agricola* has exercised a steady attraction on generation after generation of readers. The subject – the early history of our own island – has a strong natural appeal. The style often sparkles, and is never dull or sluggish. Deep in the heart of the book lies an ideal that commands admiration – belief in Rome, in Roman destiny, and in the Roman ways and standards of life. There is a note of tragedy in the thought that this ideal has to live in an unfriendly world, in conditions which make it impossible for it to reach perfection. And throughout a touch of warmth is added by the true affection that Tacitus bore his father-in-law.

IV. *Tacitus's Account of Britain*

Britain was already fairly well known to the Romans by the time Tacitus began to write. Even before 300 B.C. Pytheas of Marseilles had visited the island; he published some precious details about it, but was only called a liar for his pains. Caesar, Strabo, Pomponius Mela, and others, had added their quota to the account. Tacitus had the obvious advantage of close relationship to one who knew Britain as no Roman had ever known it before. But it is hard to take him quite seriously when he claims to have put research on a new basis, with solid fact to replace guess-work. He might possibly have done so had he taken more trouble.

Tacitus still held the false belief that Britain was much nearer Spain than it actually is, and that Ireland lay between them. He accepted a false view of the shape of Britain. Certainly he could now for the first time state positively that Britain was an island – Agricola's admiral had confirmed the fact; but it had been guessed long before. It is hard again to understand how he can speak of the Orkneys as 'hitherto unknown'; 'unexplored' might be the truer word. Tacitus omits some details found in Caesar about the customs of the Britons – for example, their partiality for geese and their collective marriages –

without troubling to correct them, if they needed correction. He never mentions the Druids, never says a word about the native British coinage, though it can hardly have been obsolete by his time. He has good accounts of the climate and of the deep inland penetrations of the sea in the north. But he sends Agricola on expedition after expedition without once mentioning his base. He does not mention by name any of the chief Roman towns, such as London, Verulamium, or York. Writing for the special purpose of biography, he clearly omits much that must have figured in his *Histories*. But the achievements of Agricola, thrown onto so uncertain a background, begin to become blurred themselves. Tacitus writes as if any province, any provincials, any army, any enemy might serve equally well to illustrate his hero's virtues. Modern taste demands more precision.

v. *Britain before Agricola*

Modern archaeologists can tell us a little about the culture of Britain in the later Iron Age, but detailed knowledge only begins with Julius Caesar. That great conqueror, during his victories in Gaul, became aware of an unconquered Britain on his flank and decided to reduce it. His two expeditions – the one in 55 B.C. a mere reconnaissance in force, the second in 54 B.C. an attempt at a partial conquest – were not wholly successful. Indeed, had we any account but Caesar's own, we should perhaps regard the second expedition as a definite failure. Britain, nominally subject to tribute, remained in fact independent.

Augustus for a short time played with the idea of conquering Britain, but soon abandoned it for more serious projects. So our island remained free. But intercourse between Britain and Gaul was active and Roman influence steadily grew. Cunobelinus (Shakespeare's Cymbeline) for most of his long reign was a friend of Rome. Caligula in A.D. 39 gave a welcome to an exiled British prince and toyed with the idea of an invasion. But it was actually left to Claudius to carry out the enterprise in A.D. 43. His chief motive was the ambition to earn a 'proper triumph' (*iustus triumphus*) by adding to the empire a country which Julius Caesar had invaded without making any very serious endeavour to annex it.* Britain, though apparently in a disturbed condition, could hardly be regarded as dangerous to Rome; and if great mineral wealth was expected from it the hope was certainly disappointed.

The conquest was carried out without a hitch by Aulus Plautius. Claudius himself spent some days with his victorious army and was saluted as 'Imperator'. The south-east of Britain and Vectis (Isle of Wight) were quickly overrun. The next governor, Ostorius Scapula (47–52), fought against the Silures in South Wales, drove away the patriot leader Caratacus, son of Cunobelinus, and enforced his surrender when he fled north to the Brigantes in Yorkshire. By 49 the Romans had probably reached the Trent, Severn, and Dee, and were masters of Lincoln, Wroxeter, and Chester. Colchester now became a colony.

* Suetonius, *Divus Claudius* 17.

Under Didius Gallus (52–58) and Veranius (58) there was no serious advance. Suetonius Paulinus (58/9–61) ventured out incautiously from Chester to occupy Anglesey, but was completely surprised by a general rising in his rear. It was led by Boudicca (Boadicea), Queen of the Iceni, who had bitter private wrongs to avenge. The rebels swept all before them and overran London, Colchester, and Verulamium. The cause of Rome looked desperate. But Paulinus, hastening back, brought the enemy to battle somewhere in the Midlands and retrieved everything by a single decisive victory. Paulinus was too merciless to the guilty, and the revolt dragged on. The government of Nero, therefore, showed true wisdom in replacing Paulinus by the gentler Petronius Turpilianus. He and his successors, Trebellius Maximus and Vettius Bolanus, ruled mildly during the years 61–71. The province as a whole was at peace, but the armies were mutinous.

Petilius Cerealis, one of Vespasian's ablest generals, showed great vigour and made good progress with the conquest of the Brigantes in Yorkshire (71–74). Undaunted by his great reputation, his successor Julius Frontinus (74–78) broke the resistance of the Silures in South Wales.

vi. *Agricola's Governorship*

It was almost certainly in A.D. 78 that Agricola succeeded Frontinus in Britain.

His seven campaigns may be summarized as follows:

(1) A.D. 78. Defeat of the Ordovices in North Wales. Conquest of Anglesey.

(2) A.D. 79. Advance northwards by western route from Chester and York. North-west England consolidated by forts and garrisons.

(3) A.D. 80. Advance northwards by eastern route, penetrating, at the farthest, as far north as the Tay.

(4) A.D. 81. Consolidation of Forth–Clyde line by establishment of forts (Camelon, Croy Hill, Bar Hill, etc.).

(5) A.D. 82. Advance along west coast from Solway Firth to Galloway peninsula and Ayrshire. Invasion of Ireland possibly contemplated, certainly not carried out.

(6) A.D. 83. Advance through coastal areas around and to the north of the Tay, with co-operation of fleet. Caledonians attack forts and try to storm camp of ninth legion. A cohort of Usipi mutinies and sails round North Britain.

(7) A.D. 84. Advance to neighbourhood of Moray Firth. Crushing defeat of Caledonians at Mons Graupius. Agricola recalled in the same year.

Readers will observe how much geographical detail has to be added to make Tacitus's account intelligible.

VII. *Britain after Agricola*

Tacitus tells us (*Histories* I, 2) that Britain had been 'completely conquered and then immediately let go'. This refers to the fact that a few years after Agricola's recall a legion was withdrawn from the province, to help in dealing with troubles elsewhere, and some of his permanent forts in Perthshire were evacuated and demolished. But this does not mean that all Agricola's gains were abandoned. Some of his Scottish forts appear to have still been held early in the reign of Trajan. In A.D. 122 and the following years Hadrian built his famous wall from the Tyne to the Solway; and in 142 Antoninus Pius built a wall from the Forth to the Clyde.

III. *The Army of Britain*

Britain was occupied, after the Claudian conquest, by four legions – II Augusta, IX Hispana, XIV Gemina, and XX Valeria – with the usual addition of auxiliary forces. Of these legions, the following were still in Britain at the time of Agricola's arrival:

>Legio II Augusta (at Caerleon)
>Legio IX Hispana (at York)
>Legio XX Valeria

A fourth legion, II Adiutrix, had replaced XIV Gemina in A.D. 71, and was now stationed at Chester. Among the auxiliary troops in Britain we can identify four cohorts of Batavi and two of Tungri which fought at Mons Graupius, a cohort of Usipi that deserted and sailed round North Britain, and perhaps one or more cohorts of Britons. Tacitus does not mention the name of a single one of Agricola's justly famous permanent forts. A number of these, however, have been identified after careful excavation – especially those at Fendoch (at the mouth of the Sma' Glen in Perthshire) and at Inchtuthil (on the north bank of the Tay, eleven miles north of Perth). When Legio II Adiutrix was withdrawn from Britain (perhaps as early as A.D. 87), Legio XX Valeria was moved from Scotland into England and some of these forts abandoned.

IX. Germania, the Book

Tacitus's essay 'On the Origin and Geography of Germany' was long ago hailed as a 'golden book'. It is certainly the best of its kind in antiquity, perhaps in any age. The genius of the author has stamped it with a character of its own; but none the less it follows a model that had gradually been developed over many centuries.

Here as always it is to Greece that one must look first. Hecataeus of Miletus, Herodotus, the great medical writer Hippocrates, and Aristotle himself, had found time for the study of peoples. Coming to Roman times, we find Posidonius of Rhodes (c. 135–50 B.C.) devoting to Germany the thirtieth of his fifty-two books of histories. First among the Roman authors comes Julius Caesar, who allotted a few invaluable chapters of his *Gallic War* to the German peoples. Livy devoted the 104th book of his histories to an account of Germany. He must have been able to draw on fresh sources of information, opened up by the campaigns of Augustus's generals in Germany. Strabo wrote of Germany in his seventh book; but he is thought to have been little known or studied in the West. Pliny the Elder carried his *German Wars* down to about

the death of Claudius. It was obviously a work of the
first importance, but it is completely lost. Pliny had
served on the frontier himself, and so could depend on
personal observation, as well as on the evidence of friends.
Tacitus certainly knew and esteemed the work of Caesar.
Strabo, perhaps, was unfamiliar to him. Tacitus's debt to
Pliny would probably prove to be very great, could we
assess it exactly. How much Tacitus may have been able
to add by drawing on the experience of soldiers and
merchants of his own day cannot be exactly gauged, but
it must have been considerable.

The date of the *Germania* is exactly fixed in A.D. 98, the
second consulship of Trajan. It is only a very little later
than the *Agricola* and may even have overlapped it in
composition.

The *Germania* is, as it professes to be, a study of the
character, customs, and geography of a people. But is it
something more than that – a tract with a definite moral
purpose, or a political pamphlet? It is necessary to exam-
ine these questions before going on to another one – is the
Germania, in general, reliable?

Tacitus unmistakably contrasts the virtues of the
Germans, which recall the uncorrupted morals of old
Rome, with the degeneracy of the Empire. The Germans
think lightly of the precious metals. They love freedom.
Freedmen are kept in their proper place. Women are
chaste, home-life is pure, childlessness is not turned into a
profitable career. There are no lascivious banquets, no
professional shows, no pompous funerals. Many a biting

epigram sharpens the contrast: 'No one in Germany calls it "up-to-date" to seduce and be seduced.' On the other hand, they are not completely idealized. Their characteristic weaknesses are exposed – their indolence, their quarrelsomeness, their drunkenness, their silly passion for war.

The tendency to moralize, then, is a feature, but not the main purpose, of the book. The suggestion left on the mind of the reader is that, if the Empire should continue to relax in so deep a peace and if the Germans should add discipline to their valour, they would become a deadly menace to Rome. Tacitus was certainly speaking with the voice of history herself.

The emperor Trajan spent the first year or so of his reign in the two German provinces*, and was still there when the *Germania* came out. Tacitus obviously took advantage of the popular interest in those provinces. But was he venturing to recommend any definite policy, either that of the emperor himself or an alternative one?

The policy of Trajan, possibly not obvious at the time, became so as his reign went on. The German frontier was to be firmly held, but there was to be no conquest of Germany. The strength of the Roman arms was to be directed against Dacia and Parthia. Now, what does Tacitus say? The conquest of Germany is taking so long – too long. All that Rome can now pray for is that her enemies may be disunited. There is no suggestion of a

* 'Upper' and 'Lower' Germany, military districts on the *left* bank of the Rhine.

renewed offensive. The one allusion to the Elbe is just a
sigh of regret over a dream of the past. For all that,
Germany cannot be treated lightly: unconquered, she
remains a constant challenge and a constant threat to
Rome.

So far, the suggestions of Tacitus seem to point in the
same direction as the official policy, but they do not go
with it all the way. When he speaks of destiny driving
the Roman empire upon its appointed path (Chapter
33), he seems to imply a more pessimistic view than
Trajan would have been likely to take. For Tacitus the
best is over: fortune has already given Rome her choicest
gifts. Trajan showed by his actions that he judged the
extension of the empire to be both possible and desirable.
One passage in the *Germania* (Chapter 37) reads like a
deliberate criticism of the policy which Trajan was later
to pursue: the freedom of the Germans, Tacitus implies,
may well prove more formidable than the despotism of
the Parthian kings.

Tacitus, then, realizes the political interest of his subject
and gives fair expression to some of the considerations
that governed official policy; but he is not a propagandist,
and in any case the political aspect is subordinated to the
main theme.

To the question whether the *Germania* is reliable we
can give on the whole an affirmative answer. Tacitus is at
fault here and there: for example, he underrates the
importance of Roman trade with Germany and exag-
gerates the German disregard for gold and silver. But his

evidence on many points – such as German armour and dress – has been brilliantly confirmed by archaeological evidence. If he sometimes applies to the Germans phrases applied by earlier authors to other peoples, he does not borrow slavishly or in ignorance. Where the Germans differ, he is quick to note the difference.

The German people in the time of Tacitus was already a force to be reckoned with in Europe. We know to our cost that it has not ceased to be so today. Has Tacitus fairly characterized the Germans of his time? And do their characteristics live on in the Germany of today?

Tacitus's picture of the Germans is vivid and consistent. They have a strong love of freedom, a keen sense of honour, and a regard for the sanctity of home-life. They possess the military virtues, but make them look somewhat ridiculous by wanting to fight for any or no reason. In peace-time their standards relax abruptly. In fact, they are like adventurous lads, never quite grown up. They need Roman discipline if they are ever to reach maturity. Tacitus's claim for a unique purity of the race may be exaggerated, but is not altogether at fault. He never dreamt of the mischievous nonsense that he was going to suggest to later theorists.

What might the future of Europe have been if Augustus had held the Elbe frontier and made Germany a Roman province? Modern Germany has claimed to draw her strength from her ancient barbarian tradition, and has made a virtue of her late submission to Latin civilization. She has glorified the natural man with all his virtues and his vices. The *Germania* has been brought into this movement. It has been assiduously taught in German schools and universities and made into a sort of Bible of German patriotism.

The population of Germany has certainly changed very considerably since the time of Tacitus. The real Nordic race must surely be sought first in Scandinavia, if anywhere. The National Socialist talk of 'Blut und Boden' was just mystical nonsense. One cannot really make heroic models out of the boisterous, overgrown boys that the ancient Germans were. All these appeals to ancient history to justify modern policies begin with self-deception and proceed to deceive others. Races do not remain pure over centuries. Whatever the fanatic may say, the disinterested student will have none of it. But climate does remain much the same over millennia, and can profoundly influence the character of peoples. Is it possible, then, that the 'Germanentum', the fierce sense of national idiosyncracy, the 'Furor Teutonicus', may be something that really tends to grow in the various peoples that have successively fallen under the influence of 'Middle Europe'? Well, that will be one of the inevitable causes to which the fatalist will attribute the fall of Europe, if Europe really is to fall. But we have still the right to hope that more self-knowledge and more self-discipline can save Germany and Europe together.

On a few points Tacitus seems to be in error – for instance, when he denies that domestic slavery existed in Germany. His account of the German chiefs is quite correct, if we understand by 'chiefs' the men marked out by birth and wealth as natural leaders. To make them out to be magistrates raises unnecessary difficulties.

In several passages Tacitus speaks of 'the hundred' in technical senses which modern scholars have found hard to understand; but the suggestion that he misunderstood the word 'hundreds' – used, it is alleged, by his authorities in the sense of subdivisions of German states – will not do. Neither in Germany nor in Anglo-Saxon England was the word so used till centuries later.

x. *Germany and Rome in History*

For long centuries the German peoples were pressed back in the north-west from Jutland to the Oder by the masses of Gauls, who were then superior to them in strength. The civilized world confused them with the Gauls. In time they began to roam westward, and the Tungri and other tribes established themselves on the left bank of the Rhine. Rome, however, never realized who the Germans were, until in 113 B.C. the Cimbri and Teutoni emigrated from their far northern homes and broke in upon Italy. They first appeared to the north-east, and won a victory over a Roman consul; then, after wander'ng about on the north of the Alps for four years they invaded the Rhone valley and defeated two consuls. Worse was still to come. In 105 two consular armies were destroyed at Orange. Had the barbarians advanced direct on Italy, no one knows what might have happened. As it was, they turned aside to conquer Spain, found the

Spanish resistance unexpectedly tough, and returned to Gaul three years later. Rome had had time to rally, and her best general, Marius, had given a new discipline and spirit to the army. The barbarians divided their forces. The Teutoni were destroyed by Marius at Aix-en-Provence. The Cimbri, who had crossed over to enter Italy from the east, were crushed at Vercellae in the next year. The storm died down as suddenly as it had sprung up.

For over forty years the Germans remained quiet. But in 58 Julius Caesar encountered a new menace in Ariovistus, King of the Suebi. He had been invited by Gallic tribes to help them against rivals, but soon took hostages and exacted tribute from his friends and kept drawing in new war-bands from Germany. Caesar picked a quarrel with him and drove him in rout across the Rhine. But Ariovistus had been accepted as a 'friend' by the Roman Senate, and Caesar's enemies in Rome accused him of downright treachery.

Again followed a long interval of peace. During the whole of the great civil wars the Germans made no move. Augustus, when he had won supreme power, turned his attention to the dangerous north. Not satisfied with the Rhine as a frontier, he decided on an advance to the Elbe. In a series of campaigns, directed by the stepsons of Augustus, Nero Drusus and Tiberius, the Germans were defeated in war, and were then gradually inured to Roman ways. It seemed to be only a matter of a few years before Germany would be made a province of the empire. But the Romans' attention was distracted by the dangerous ambitions of Maroboduus, king of the Marcomanni in the south-east. Close on this followed a desperate revolt against Roman rule in Illyricum and Pannonia. Germany was left in charge of P. Quinctilius Varus, a nobleman devoid of military talent. He was ambushed and destroyed with his three legions in the *Teutoburgiensis Saltus* by Arminius (Hermann), chief of the Cherusci (A.D. 9). Augustus, brooding in bitterness, was often heard to cry out to Varus to 'give him back his legions'. Rome now returned to the defensive. Arminius himself, aspiring to kingship, was destroyed by his enemies at home. But he had done something very difficult. He had diverted the Romans from a plan deliberately resolved on. From 14 to 16 Tiberius allowed his adoptive son Germanicus to make some amends for the disaster of Varus by displaying the Roman arms and paying honours to the Roman dead in the fatal forest. But a conquest would obviously cost too much. Tiberius decided to keep the empire within its existing frontiers. Caligula suddenly conceived, and as suddenly dropped, a grandiose scheme of German conquest. Peace continued with hardly a break. But in the civil wars of 68–69 a Batavian nobleman, Civilis, roused his countrymen, under cloak of loyalty to Vespasian, against Vitellius. The movement was joined by other German tribes and the Roman armies on the Rhine became demoralized. On the death of Vitellius in December 69, Civilis should have placed himself at the disposal of Vespasian. But his head was turned. Some of the Gallic tribes broke loose from Rome and proclaimed an 'Empire of the Gauls'. The Germans naturally knew who would be the real masters if the revolt succeeded. But Vespasian struck swiftly and remorselessly. His general Cerealis soon won a considerable victory; the Gauls of the south decided, on consideration, to remain loyal to Rome, and the rebels in the north began to waver. Civilis was content to accept surrender on reasonable terms; but Vespasian was inexorable in obliterating every trace of that ominous Gallic Empire. He and his sons tried to insure against future troubles. They narrowed the dangerous gap between Rhine and Danube by occupying the *Agri Decumates* (see Chapter 29) and drawing a military frontier for their defence. Domitian fought bitter wars on the middle Rhine against the Chatti in 83 and 89. Though it was the fashion at Rome to deride his 'sham triumphs', modern archaeology has shown that his success was not inconsiderable.

Trajan was in command in the Upper German province when he was adopted by Nerva, and he administered the two provinces in 98–99. It was probably in 98 that the Bructeri were nearly wiped out by their German enemies. Trajan left the frontier so secure that legions could be transferred from Rhine to Danube.

So far we have been speaking of the western Germans. With the eastern Germans Rome's relations began later and were less close. In 8 B.C. the Marcomanni and Quadi drove the Boii out of Bohemia. Maroboduus, the great Marcomannic king, gathered round him so large a confederacy as to excite Rome's suspicions (*c.* A.D. 6). But his glory excited the envy of the other Germans; his empire collapsed and he finally accepted sanctuary at Ravenna in A.D. 19. The troubles on the Danube under Domitian were caused, not so much by the Germans, as by the Dacians and Sarmatians. The terrible wars of Marcus Aurelius against the Quadi and Marcomanni lie beyond our present scope.

History in the main has justified the forebodings of Tacitus. Germany, often triumphed over, was never conquered. The time came when no skill in defence, no valour in the field, no subtlety in diplomacy – and finally not even the discord among the Germans themselves – could avail. Destiny at last pressed the empire too hard. The barriers broke and the barbarian tides flooded in.

XI. *The Early Roman Empire*

The Roman Republic throve just so long as the Senate was able to direct and co-ordinate its policy. It broke down when the Senate lost control of its provincial governors and of its generals and their devoted but rapacious armies. In the last and deadliest of the civil wars in which the breakdown resulted, Julius Caesar won supreme power under the title of Dictator. His clear intention of ruling as an autocrat led to his murder on the famous Ides of March (15 March, 44 B.C.).

The death of Caesar was followed by thirteen years of chaos. The attempt of Brutus and Cassius to restore the Republic failed. Then the leaders of the Caesarian faction partitioned the state between them. Finally it came to a life-and-death struggle between young Caesar (Octavian), grand-nephew and son by adoption of the dictator, and Mark Antony, with his Egyptian wife, Queen Cleopatra. The naval battle of Actium (31 B.C.) decided the issue in favour of the young Caesar.

Octavian was determined to succeed where Julius Caesar had failed: no assassins' daggers for him. He 'restored' the Republic, but built into it a new position for himself, thus founding what we have learnt to call the Empire. He established peace and order throughout the Roman world. He soon abandoned the idea of conquering Britain, but tried long and hard to establish a province of Germany on the right bank of the Rhine. The failure of this scheme has been described above. In the east he forced the Parthian king to restore the Roman standards captured at Carrhae in 53 B.C., and he asserted Roman suzerainty over Armenia. The mere threat of war sufficed to restore Roman honour.

As early as 27 B.C. he received the title of Augustus ('Revered'), by which we still know him. His ever-growing prestige was still more fully recognized when he was named 'Father of his country' in 2 B.C. But if his work was to outlive him he must find a suitable successor, and to this end he laboured long and earnestly. First his nephew Marcellus, then his great captain Agrippa, then Agrippa's sons, Gaius and Lucius Caesar, who were adopted by Augustus himself, seemed destined for the succession. In the end, when all the rest had died, it was his step-son Tiberius who shared with him the burdens of empire and stood ready to take them over at his death in A.D. 14.

The long reign of Tiberius was marked by sound administration and sober foreign policy, based on that of Augustus. A renewed attempt to conquer Germany was abandoned in 17. Apart from that war and local risings in Gaul and Africa, the world enjoyed a golden age of peace. But at Rome Tiberius was never popular. Suspicious and uncertain of himself, he allowed the charge of high treason to be abused by informers against men of mark. And there was a constant struggle over the succession. Germanicus, nephew of Tiberius, died in 19; his own son Drusus in 23. In the following years Sejanus, the powerful praetorian prefect, succeeded in poisoning Tiberius's mind against Agrippina the widow of Germanicus and her family. Her two eldest sons, Nero and Drusus, were disgraced and put to death, and she herself died in exile. Tiberius meanwhile had withdrawn to the lovely island of Capri – to live, so rumour said, a life the reverse of lovely – and Sejanus was left to lord it over Rome. Still not content, he plotted against Tiberius. But the emperor, warned just in time, struck first, and Sejanus fell (31). Tiberius never returned to Rome but died, unloved and despondent, in 37.

Gaius was the youngest son of Germanicus, taken into favour at the last by his great-uncle. He had been born in camp and still bears the nickname of Caligula ('Little Boot') given him by the soldiers. Having cringed to the aged Tiberius, he now delighted to play the tyrant, and not content even with tyranny he affected to be a god on earth. His ambitious schemes of conquest in Germany and Britain merely made him look foolish. He was eventually murdered in 41 by an old army officer whom he had made a practice of insulting.

Gaius left no obvious successor, and the Senate seriously debated a restoration of the Republic. But the praetorian guards had found in the palace the middle-aged uncle of Gaius, the eccentric Claudius, and soon decided that he was not too eccentric for them. The Senate had no choice but to submit. Claudius was slow and pedantic, a slightly ridiculous character, but nevertheless able and conscientious. He carried through with complete success the long-discussed conquest of Britain (43). He was derided by the Romans, not without some justification, as the slave of his wives and freedmen. His third wife – his niece Agrippina the Younger – established a complete ascendancy over him. She induced him to adopt her own son by a previous marriage, L. Domitius Ahenobarbus (the future emperor Nero), to marry him to his daughter Octavia, and to prefer him above his own son Britannicus. When Claudius died suddenly in 54, after eating freely of his favourite dish of mushrooms, Agrippina was with good reason regarded as his murderess.

Agrippina intended to govern with her sixteen years old son Nero, but was quietly edged out of power by the young emperor's advisers. To begin with, Nero was popular and promised well. But he soon embarked on a terrible series of family murders – first Britannicus, then Agrippina, then his wife Octavia, whom he divorced in order to marry the 'imperial whore' Poppaea. Under the influence of the infamous praetorian prefect Tigellinus, he plunged into a career of debauchery, waste, and cruelty. 'Rome burned while Nero fiddled', and the Christians were persecuted on the pretence that they were responsible for the fire. His foreign policy had some successes – a long war with Parthia carried to a triumphant conclusion, and the British revolt under Boudicca suppressed – though a serious rising of the Jews in 66 was still not quite crushed at the end of the reign. The declaration of the freedom of Greece was at least an impressive gesture. But Rome was weary of the emperor's misgovernment and profoundly shocked by that artistic temperament which drove him to appear on the public stage. Vindex, governor of Gallia Lugdunensis, revolted, and Galba in Spain joined him. The German army under Verginius Rufus crushed Vindex, and the movement looked like collapsing. But Nero, despairing of his own cause, retired from Rome to a suburb and after long hesitation – constantly exclaiming 'What an artist the world is losing in me!' – he at last committed suicide on hearing that the Senate had declared him a public enemy.

A secret of empire had now been divulged: an emperor need not necessarily be made in Rome. Galba soon made his way to the capital and was accepted without question. But he was old, he was mean, and he lost sympathy by unnecessary cruelties and by subservience to unworthy friends. At the beginning of 69 the German armies refused to swear allegiance to him and found an emperor of their own in the person of Vitellius, governor of Lower Germany. Galba tried to prop his falling throne by adopting as his son a young nobleman, Piso. But in so doing he mortally offended another partisan, Otho, who had hoped for promotion himself. Otho bribed the praetorian guard, who promptly murdered Galba and Piso in the streets of Rome.

For most Romans the choice between Otho and Vitellius seemed to be simply one between two evils. It was the armies that decided; and the armies of Germany, led by Vitellius's lieutenants Valens and Caecina, were too much for Otho's praetorians and army of Italy. The troops serving in the Balkans and Judaea had no time to intervene; for Otho lost heart and committed suicide. But Vitellius was not left long in enjoyment of empire. Vespasian was proclaimed emperor by his soldiers in Judaea, and the Balkan armies joined him. A sudden dash on Italy by one of their captains, Antonius Primus, led to a surprise victory at Cremona over the flower of the German armies. Vitellius, betrayed by many of his friends, wished to retire; but bitter fighting broke out in Rome between his men and friends of Vespasian, and when Primus forced his way into the city and decided the issue, Vitellius was murdered in the streets.

Vespasian showed himself master of the situation. He

restored Roman prestige and repaired her shattered finances. It was hard that he should be called a miser for his pains. We have already seen how he suppressed the revolt of Civilis and the 'Empire of the Gauls', and later, in 78, sent Agricola to Britain. From the first he marked out his two sons as his heirs. Titus was admitted to a share in the government, and even Domitian, the younger son, received the title of 'prince' (*Caesar*). Titus succeeded his father in 79, and was hailed as the 'darling of the human race' for his friendliness and generosity. But he died in 81, before his qualities had been severely tested. His short reign was marked by two disasters – a great fire at Rome and the eruption of Vesuvius.

Domitian was a man of considerable ability, but of cruel and difficult temperament. He allowed the charge of high treason to be revived for use by informers against his many political enemies, and made the Senate share in the odium of their condemnation. His wars against the Chatti on the middle Rhine were not the failure that his enemies made them out to be, but his later years were darkened by long and difficult campaigns on the Danube against Sarmatians and Dacians, ending in a somewhat inglorious peace. Agricola was recalled from his victories in Britain in 84. By 96 Domitian, already hated by most people in Rome, had become suspect to his wife and his immediate entourage. To protect their own lives they assassinated him and called Nerva, an elderly lawyer of repute, to the empty throne.

Nerva showed praiseworthy intentions of restoring good government after the oppressions of Domitian. Tacitus could hail his succession as the dawn of a new age of liberty. But the praetorian guards, who had not ceased to regret Domitian, demanded his murderers for execution. Nerva pleaded, wept – and gave way. To redeem his fallen prestige he adopted Trajan, the pride of the army, as his son, and the disorderly praetorians were soon brought back to obedience. On Nerva's death in 98 Trajan was accepted without question as his successor. Trajan's long reign (98–117) was signalized by the conquest of Dacia and by a long war against Parthia, beginning with brilliant success, but compromised at the last by a general revolt of the Jews throughout the east. Early in the reign of his successor Hadrian, Tacitus died. Whether the high hopes that he had conceived in the first years of Nerva and Trajan stayed with him to the last, we cannot say. The gloomy tone of his last work, the *Annals*, suggests that he had ceased to believe in that reconciliation of autocracy with freedom of which he had so confidently written.

From Augustus to Nero the Empire was, as it were, the inheritance of a single family, the Julio–Claudian. Galba, Otho, and Vitellius stand as isolated figures. The Flavian dynasty of Vespasian expired with the death of Domitian. With Nerva began that great line of emperors, succeeding one another by adoption, which gave Rome good government for a large part of a century. It might count as a substitute for freedom – to quote Tacitus's phrase –

that emperors now began to be chosen with a sense of responsibility.

XII. *The Constitution of the Empire*

For the Romans themselves the Empire was still the Roman 'Republic' – the 'Senate and People of Rome'. But there was a modification which seems to us vital. A number of powers were conferred on one man sufficient to place him at the head of the state and to make his authority everywhere decisive.

In the first place the emperor was *imperator*, holder of the supreme right of military command. The armies swore allegiance to him and to no one else. In the second place, as holder of tribunician power, he represented the Roman people, was personally inviolable, and could convene the Senate and initiate legislation. Further powers might be granted to a princeps by special enactment or assumed by him *ad hoc* to deal with a particular situation. Some such powers were defined in a *lex de imperio* which was enacted upon Vespasian's accession; and in A.D. 73 he also revived the censorship, which Domitian held continuously for the last ten or more years of his reign.

Those provinces which required armies were administered for the emperor by his representatives; and even in the peaceful provinces which were left to the Senate he had power to intervene at discretion. In Rome and Italy, which in theory were under the control of the Senate, he undertook special duties, such as the charge of the corn-supply, of the night-watch, and occasionally of the public roads. He was sometimes specially entrusted with the supervision of public morals. He had his own treasury, the *fiscus*, as well as a special military treasury. He struck gold and silver coins in his own right; the coinage in base metal was administered by the Senate, but always under his supervision. He could dispense justice in other courts as well as in a High Court of his own. The expressions of his will, given in edicts, dispatches, and the like, came more and more to have the full force of laws. As *pontifex maximus* (chief priest) he was head of the state religion. While he lived Rome sacrificed only to his *genius* (spirit); but in the provinces he was actually worshipped as a god. After death, unless his memory was condemned, he was consecrated, became *Divus* (the divine), and received full religious honours.

To help him in his great task he drew on all classes of society – on the Senate for his chief provincial governors and generals; on the *equites* (Knights) for his junior officers and financial agents (procurators); on the freedmen for the heads of such departments of his court as finance, correspondence, and petitions (*a rationibus, ab epistulis, a libellis*); on the slaves for the lower posts of his bureaux. As Senate and Knights were so essential to his service, he found means of controlling the composition of both these Orders.

The emperor normally tried to fix the succession by marking out a son or other close relative, or a son by adoption, as his political heir. The title *Augustus*, conferred on the first emperor in 27 B.C., was borne by all his successors. *Caesar*, in origin the family name of Julius, was taken over by most emperors; but it was sometimes used to designate an heir or prince. *Princeps* (chief citizen) was a common, though unofficial, designation of the emperor.

The Senate was taken by the emperor into partnership. It had the general control of Rome, Italy, and the peaceful provinces, and, acting on the emperor's initiative, transacted a mass of public business by its decrees (*senatus consulta*). It administered the old state treasury, the *aerarium Saturni*. It even acquired powers unknown to it during the Republic. It took over from the people the election of magistrates and sat as a High Court of Justice. It was the Senate alone that could make an emperor's position fully constitutional. The army could sometimes confer power, but could never legitimize it. It was the Senate alone that judged the emperor's record after his death. Yet the partnership – the 'dyarchy', or 'rule of two', as it has been called – was always an unequal one: for in the last resort the emperor held the power of the sword.

The Roman people ceased to exercise its rights directly. It looked to the emperor to represent and protect it. A Roman satirist bitterly observed that its real requirements were two – *panem et circenses* (bread and games).

The old Republican magistrates continued to be elected yearly. A man would enter the Senate as quaestor, would then become tribune or aedile, next praetor, and finally consul. The quaestors had financial duties in Rome,

Italy, and the provinces. The aediles were in charge of buildings and the police in Rome; the tribunes were still champions of the people, but were dwarfed by the emperor's tribunician power. The praetors retained only a part of their original legal functions, but were given the showy and expensive charge of holding the public games.

The consuls were still the chief magistrates of Rome, and the two regular consuls of each year (*ordinarii*) gave their names to it.* The office was now limited to a few months, and many extra consuls (*suffecti*) were appointed. By nominating and commending candidates the emperor kept a firm control of elections. Prominent among the new officers created by the Empire were the prefect of Rome, a senator nominated by the emperor, and the prefect of the praetorian guard, a Knight.

xiii. *The Provinces of the Empire*

The Roman empire was divided into a number of spheres of administration or, as we still call them, provinces. It was in the main the creation of the Republic. The emperors consolidated it and rounded it off at the edges, but only rarely added new provinces.

The provinces where armies were required were governed by deputies appointed by the emperor, his legates, men of either praetorian or consular rank. There were other legates to command the legions, others to assist the governor in his duties. A financial officer – the

---

* The emperor would at intervals open the year as 'ordinary' consul with a colleague.

procurator – attended to finance. A few minor provinces had no legate, but were under procurators who were also governors: such a one was Pontius Pilate, procurator of Judaea, under whom our Lord suffered. Egypt had its prefect, or viceroy.

The senatorial provinces – those that were peaceful and unarmed – were governed by officers appointed by the Senate: Africa and Asia by proconsuls, the rest by pro-praetors. The financial officer here was the quaestor; the procurator simply looked after imperial interests.

Every province was divided into 'dioceses' or administrative districts and *conventus* – smaller districts in which the assizes were held. There were provincial councils to represent provincial interests, but they do not seem to have attained any great political importance. Taxes were assessed either as lump sums or as quotas levied on natural produce. Collection was at first indirect, but tended to become direct as time went on. The burden of taxation was, according to ancient standards, not heavy. But there were also levies of corn and the like, often aggravated by cruel and absurd abuses.

Rome tended to rest her rule on the cities and, in the cities, on the moneyed classes. Some favoured communities became Roman colonies, others *municipia* – that is to say, corporations organized on the old Italian model. A few cities – Athens, for example – remained nominally free. The population of the empire cannot be closely estimated. It may have been 40 or 50 millions in the reign of Augustus.

Short notes on the provinces mentioned in the text will be found in the Glossary.

XIV. *The Army and Fleet of the Empire*

The armies of the empire consisted of the regulars composing the legions and of auxiliary troops. They were stationed chiefly on the frontiers, and served for defence rather than for attack. There was no field army.

The legion was a brigade, consisting of foot, horse, and auxiliary services. It was divided into ten cohorts; the cohort was divided into three maniples, the maniple into two centuries. The strength of the legion was about 5,500 men. The legate, or brigadier, was a senator appointed by the emperor. Under him were *tribuni militum* – young men starting on a Senatorial or Equestrian career. But the discipline and efficiency of a legion depended mainly on its centurions, sixty in number. The first centurion in each cohort was called *pilus prior*; and the *pilus prior* of the first cohort in each legion – brigade sergeant-major – was called *primipilus*. The centurions' staff of office was a cudgel of vinewood (*vitis*) – not intended only for ornament. The standard of the legion was a silver eagle (*aquila*). The maniples had their own standards (*signa*). A flag (*vexillum*) was used by squadrons of cavalry, by corps of veterans, and by detachments of infantry employed on special duties.

The term of service was fixed by Augustus at sixteen years, later raised to twenty. The pay – 300 *denarii* a year – was raised by one-third under Domitian. A special military treasury, founded in A.D. 6, provided for veterans. The legions were recruited at first from a few nearby provinces, later more widely. In theory at least only Roman citizens were eligible. Conscription could at any time be applied, but voluntary enlistment usually sufficed. Under Augustus there were twenty-five legions; by the end of the second century the number had risen to thirty-three.

The auxiliary troops were recruited in the provinces, chiefly in those that were new and warlike. They often used native weapons, but were usually employed away from home. They obtained Roman citizenship on discharge. The auxiliary infantry was organized in cohorts of 1,000 or 500 men, commanded by colonels (*praefecti cohortis*) of Equestrian rank; the cavalry in squadrons of the same numbers, similarly commanded by colonels (*praefecti alae*). The auxiliaries received their keep, but nothing is known of their pay.

The garrison of Rome was composed of three parts. Its *corps d'élite* – the praetorian guard, concentrated by Tiberius in one camp at Rome – was recruited from Italy and some of the more Romanized provinces. It consisted of nine cohorts. Its commander (*praefectus praetorio*) had under him tribunes and centurions. The pay and the prestige of the praetorians were higher than those of the legionaries, their term of service shorter. The urban cohorts, four (later seven) in number, were under the command of a senator (*praefectus urbi*). Not all these cohorts were stationed in Rome: one, for example, was at

Lugdunum (Lyons) as guard of the imperial mint there. The watch (*vigiles*), in seven cohorts, were freedmen commanded by a Knight (*praefectus vigilum*). Both urban cohorts and watch had their own tribunes and centurions.

The fleet was decidedly an inferior service. The captains (*trierarchae*) and the men (*classiarii*) were usually of free birth but not Romans. The admirals (*praefecti classis*) might be Knights, but even freedmen were sometimes appointed. The ships in use were mainly the quinquereme, the trireme, and the fast light Liburnian galley. Italy had two main fleets, stationed at Ravenna and Misenum; but there were many subordinate fleets throughout the empire – fleets of the Rhine, the Danube, and the Black Sea, fleets of Egypt and of Britain. It was a Roman, Pompey the Great, who invented the slogan *navigare necesse est, vivere non est necesse* – 'keep the seas we must, live if we can'. But in general his fellow-countrymen did little to live up to it.

BRITANNIA

English Miles
0 10 20 30 40 50

■ Legionary Fortresses
□ Forts
■ Forts certainly or probably
    established before A.D 110
⊙ Large Towns
○ Small Towns (and modern names)

Forfar

Perth ·Tava Aest.

CALEDONIA ·Bodotria Aest.

Camelon *Inveresk*
Castledykes Tweed
Clyde Trimontium
            (*Newstead*)
Clota Aest. Cappuck

Birrens

Hadrian's Wall Tyne
Ituna Aest. Corstopium
Luguvallium ·Tyne
(*Carlisle*)
Uxelodunuma Brocavum
(*Maryport*)

Monapia *Lancaster* Eburacum
                        (*York*)
                Ilkley Abus Aest.
Wigan *Castleshaw* Cambodunum?
Canovium *Manchester* Lindum (*Lincoln*)
(*Caerhun*)
Segontium Mona Deva *Derby* Metaris Aest.
(*Carnarvon*) (*Chester*) Trisantona? Venta
            Dee Viroconium Ratae Durobrivae Icenorum
Caersws   (*Leicester*) *Peterborough*
                Watling ICENI
Castell Collen *Huntingdon*
            Cambridge
Gaer Ceelbren Lexden Camulodunum
Maridunum Glevum Verulamium
Gellygaer Penydarren (*St Albans*) Dorchester TRINOVANTES
S Isca Venta Corinium Londinium Tamesa Aest.
  (*Caerleon*)   Staines
Cardiff Aquae Sulis Calleva Durovernum Rutupiae
Sabrina Aest.   CANTI Dubrae
            BELGAE Venta Belgarum Anderida
                    Portus Lemanis
        Durnovaria
DUMNONII   Vectis Gessoriacum
    Moridunum (*I. of Wight*) (*Boulogne*)
    (*Seaton*)
Isca Dumnoniorum
(*Exeter*)

AGRICOLA

1

FAMOUS men of old often had their lives and characters set on record; and even our generation, with all its indifference to the world around it, has not quite abandoned the practice. An outstanding personality can still triumph over that blind antipathy to virtue which is a defect of all states, small and great alike. In the past, however, the road to memorable achievement was not so uphill or so beset with obstacles, and the task or recording it never failed to attract men of genius. There was no question of partiality or self-seeking. The consciousness of an honourable aim was reward enough. Many even felt that to tell their own life's story showed self-confidence rather than conceit. When Rutilius and Scaurus did so, they were neither disbelieved nor criticized; for noble character is best appreciated in those ages in which it can most readily develop. But in these times, when I planned to recount the life of one no longer with us I had to crave an indulgence which I should not have sought for an invective. So savage and hostile to merit was the age.

2

Eulogies, indeed, were written by Arulenus Rusticus and Herennius Senecio – the one, of Thrasea Paetus; the other, of Helvidius Priscus. But both were treated as capital offences, and the savage rage of their enemies was vented upon the books as well as upon their authors. The public executioners, under official instructions, made a bonfire in Comitium and Forum of those masterpieces of literary art. So much is in the record. In those fires doubtless the Government imagined that it could silence the voice of Rome and annihilate the freedom of the Senate and men's knowledge of the truth. They even went on to banish the professors of philosophy and exile all honourable accomplishments, so that nothing decent might anywhere confront them. We have indeed set up a record of subservience. Rome of old explored the utmost limits of freedom; we have plumbed the depths of slavery, robbed as we are by informers even of the right to exchange ideas in conversation. We should have lost our memories as well as our tongues had it been as easy to forget as to be silent.

3

Now at long last our spirit revives. In the first dawn of this blessed age, Nerva harmonized the old discord between autocracy and freedom; day by day Trajan is enhancing the happiness of our times; and the national security, instead of being something to be hoped and prayed for, has attained the solid assurance of a prayer fulfilled. Yet our human nature is so weak that remedies take longer to work than diseases. Our bodies, which grow so slowly, perish in the twinkling of an eye; so too the mind and its pursuits can more easily be crushed than brought to life again. Idleness gradually develops a strange fascination of its own, and we end by loving the sloth that at first we loathed. Think of it. Fifteen whole years – no small part of a man's life – taken from us. Many have died by the chance happenings of fate; all the most energetic have fallen victims to the cruelty of the emperor. And the few of us that survive are no longer what we once were, since so many of our best years have been taken from us – years in which men in their prime have aged and old men have reached the extreme limit of mortality, without ever uttering a word. Yet I shall still find some satisfaction, however inartistic and unskilled my language, in recording the bondage we once suffered, and in acknowledging the blessings we now enjoy. In the meantime, this book, which sets out to honour my father-in-law Agricola, will be commended, or at least pardoned, for the loyal affection to which it bears witness.

4

Gnaeus Julius Agricola was born in the old and famous colony of Forum Julii. Both his grandfathers were procurators in the imperial service – the crowning dignity of the Equestrian Order. His father Julius Graecinus was a member of the Senate and won fame by his devotion to literature and philosophy. By those very accomplishments he incurred the wrath of the emperor Gaius: he received orders to impeach M. Silanus, and was afterwards put to death for refusing. Agricola's mother was Julia Procilla, a paragon of feminine virtue. Brought up under her tender care, he passed his boyhood and youth in the cultivation of all the liberal arts. He was shielded from the temptations of evil companions, partly by his own sound instincts, partly by living and going to school from his very early years at Massilia, a place where Greek refinement and provincial puritanism are happily blended. I remember how he would often tell us that in his early youth he was tempted to drink deeper of philosophy than was allowable for a Roman and a future senator, but that his mother, in her wisdom, damped the fire of his passion. One can well understand that his lofty, aspiring nature was attracted strongly, if not too wisely, by the fairness and splendour of fame in its higher and nobler aspects. In time, age and discretion cooled his ardour; and he always remembered the hardest lesson that philosophy teaches – a sense of proportion.

5

He served his military apprenticeship in Britain to the satisfaction of Suetonius Paulinus, a hard-working and sensible officer, who chose him for a staff appointment in order to assess his worth. Agricola was no loose young subaltern, to turn his military career into a life of gaiety; and he would not make his staff-captaincy and his inexperience an excuse for idly enjoying himself and continually going on leave. Instead, he got to know his province and made himself known to the troops. He learned from the experts and chose the best models to follow. He never sought a duty for self-advertisement, never shirked one through cowardice. He acted always with energy and a sense of responsibility.

Neither before nor since has Britain ever been in a more disturbed and perilous state. Veterans had been massacred, colonies burned to the ground, armies cut off. They had to fight for their lives before they could think of victory. The campaign, of course, was conducted under the direction and leadership of another – the commander to whom belonged the decisive success and the credit for recovering Britain. Yet everything combined to give the young Agricola fresh skill, experience, and ambition; and his spirit was possessed by a passion for military glory – a thankless passion in an age in which a sinister construction was put upon distinction and a great reputation was as dangerous as a bad one.

6

From Britain Agricola returned to Rome to enter on his career of office, and married Domitia Decidiana, the child of an illustrious house. It was a union that brought him social distinction and aid to his ambition for advancement. They lived in rare accord, maintained by mutual affection and unselfishness; in such a partnership, however, a good wife deserves more than half the praise, just as a bad one deserves more than half the blame. On being elected quaestor, the ballot assigned him Asia as his province and Salvius Titianus as his proconsul. Neither the one nor the other corrupted him, though the province with its wealth invited abuses, and the proconsul, an abject slave to greed, was prepared to indulge his subordinate to any extent: 'You wink at my offences and I will wink at yours.' While he was in Asia a daughter was born to him, which both strengthened his position and consoled him for the loss, shortly afterwards, of a son born previously. He passed the interval between his quaestorship and his tribunate of the people, and also his year of office as tribune, in quiet retirement; for he understood the age of Nero, in which inactivity was tantamount to wisdom. His praetorship ran the same quiet course, since no judicial duties had fallen to his lot. In ordering the public games and the other vanities associated with his office, he compromised between economy and excess, steering clear of extravagance but not failing to win popular approval. He was afterwards chosen by Galba to check over the gifts in the temples; and by diligently tracing stolen objects he repaired the losses inflicted on the State by all the temple-robbers except Nero.

7

The following year dealt a grievous blow to his heart and to his family fortunes. The men of Otho's fleet, marauding at large, made a savage raid on the neighbourhood of Intimilium in Liguria, murdered Agricola's mother on her own estate, and plundered both the estate and a large part of her fortune – which was what had tempted them to commit the crime. Agricola had accordingly set out to pay the last dues of affection, when he was overtaken by the news of Vespasian's bid for Empire, and without a moment's hesitation joined his party. Mucianus was directing the inauguration of the new reign and the government of Rome; for Domitian was a very young man, to whom his father's advancement meant nothing but licence to enjoy himself. Mucianus sent Agricola to enrol recruits, and when he had performed that task with conscientious zeal put him in command of the twentieth legion. It had been slow to transfer its allegiance, and its retiring commander was reported to be disloyal. Actually, since even governors of consular rank found this legion more than they could manage and were afraid of it, the fact that a praetorian commander lacked sufficient authority to control it may well have been the soldiers' fault rather than his. Appointed, therefore, not merely to take over command, but also to mete out punishment, Agricola took disciplinary measures, but, with rare modesty, did his best to give the impression that no such measures had been necessary.

8

Britain at that time was governed by Vettius Bolanus with a hand too gentle for a warlike province. Agricola moderated his energy and restrained his enthusiasm, for fear of taking too much upon himself. He had learned the lesson of obedience and schooled himself to subordinate ambition to propriety. Shortly afterwards Petilius Cerealis, a man of consular rank, was appointed governor. Agricola now had scope to display his good qualities. But at first it was merely hard work and danger that Cerealis shared with him. The glory came later. Several times he was entrusted with a detachment of the army to test his ability; eventually, when he had passed the test, he was placed in command of larger forces. Yet he never sought to glorify himself by bragging of his achievements. It was his chief, he said, who planned all his successful operations, and he was merely the agent who executed them. Thus by his efficiency in carrying out his orders, and by his modesty in speaking of what he had done, he won distinction without arousing jealousy.

9

On Agricola's return from his military command the late emperor Vespasian granted him the status of a patrician, and afterwards placed him in charge of the province of Aquitania – a splendid promotion to an important administrative post that was a stepping-stone to the consulship, for which the emperor had in fact marked him out. It is a common belief that soldiers lack the power of fine discrimination, because the summary proceedings of a court martial – tending, as they do, to be rough and ready, and often, indeed, high-handed –

give no scope to forensic skill. But Agricola had the natural good sense, even in dealing with civilians, to show himself both agreeable and just. He made a clear division between hours of business and hours of relaxation. When the judicial duties of the assizes demanded attention, he was dignified, serious, and austere – though merciful whenever he could be. When duty had been discharged, he completely dropped his official air. As to sullenness or arrogance, he had long overcome any tendency to such faults; and he had the rare faculty of being familiar without weakening his authority and austere without forfeiting people's affection. To mention incorruptibility and strict honesty in a man of his calibre would be to insult his virtues. Even fame, which often tempts the best of men, he would not seek by self-advertisement or intrigue. He avoided all rivalry with his colleagues and all bickering with the procurators; for he considered it undignified to win such battles and ignominious to be beaten. He was kept in his post for less than three years and then called home to the immediate prospect of the consulship. Public opinion insisted that the province of Britain was being offered to him, not because he said anything himself to suggest it, but because he was obviously the right man. Rumour is not always at fault: it may even prompt a selection. During his consulship, while I was in my early manhood, he betrothed to me his daughter – a girl who already showed rare promise – and after his term of office he gave her to me in marriage. His appointment to the command of

Britain, coupled with the priestly office of a *pontifex*, followed immediately.

10

Although the geographical position and the inhabitants of Britain have been described by many authors, I shall describe them once again, not to match my industry and ability against theirs, but because the conquest was only completed in this period. Where my predecessors relied on graces of style to make their guesswork sound attractive, I shall offer ascertained fact. Britain, the largest of the islands known to us Romans, is of such a size and so situated as to run parallel to the coast of Germany on the east and to that of Spain on the west, while to the south it actually lies within sight of Gaul. Its northern shores, with no land facing them, are beaten by a wild and open sea. The general shape of Britain has been compared by Livy and by Fabius Rusticus – the finest of ancient and modern writers respectively – to an elongated diamond or a double-headed axe. Such indeed is its shape south of Caledonia, and so the same shape has been attributed to the whole. But when you go farther north you find a huge and shapeless tract of country, jutting out to form what is actually the most distant coastline and finally tapering into a kind of wedge. These remotest shores were now circumnavigated, for the first time, by a Roman fleet, which thus established the fact that Britain was an island. At the same time it discovered and sub-jugated the Orkney Islands, hitherto unknown. Thule, too, was sighted, but no more; their orders took them no farther, and winter was close at hand. But report has it that this sea is sluggish and heavy to the oar, and even in a high wind does not rise as other seas do. The reason, I suppose, is that the lands and mountains, which produce and sustain storms, are farther apart there, and the deep mass of an unbroken expanse of sea is more slowly set in motion. To investigate the nature of Ocean and its tides lies outside my subject and the matter has often been discussed. I will add just one observation. Nowhere does the sea hold wider sway: it carries to and fro in its motion a mass of tidal currents, and in its ebb and flow it does not stop at the coast, but penetrates deep inland and winds about, pushing its way even among highlands and mountains, as if in its own domain.

II

Who the first inhabitants of Britain were, whether natives or immigrants, is open to question: one must remember we are dealing with barbarians. But their physical characteristics vary, and the variation is suggestive. The reddish hair and large limbs of the Caledonians proclaim a German origin; the swarthy faces of the Silures, the tendency of their hair to curl, and the fact that Spain lies opposite, all lead one to believe that Spaniards crossed in ancient times and occupied that part of the country. The peoples nearest to the Gauls likewise resemble them. It may be that they still show the effect of a common origin; or perhaps it is climatic conditions that have produced this physical type in lands that converge so closely from north and south. On the whole, however, it seems likely that Gauls settled in the island lying so close to their shores. In both countries you find the same ritual and religious beliefs. There is no great difference in language, and there is the same hardihood in challenging danger, the same cowardice in shirking it when it comes close. But the Britons show more spirit: they have not yet been enervated by protracted peace. History tells us that the Gauls too had their hour of military glory; but since that time a life of ease has made them unwarlike: their valour perished with their freedom. The same has happened to those Britons who were conquered early; the rest are still what the Gauls once were.

12

Their strength is in their infantry. Some tribes also fight from chariots. The nobleman drives, his dependants fight in his defence. Once they owed obedience to kings; now they are distracted between the warring factions of rival chiefs. Indeed, nothing has helped us more in fighting against their very powerful nations than their inability to co-operate. It is but seldom that two or three states unite to repel a common danger; thus, fighting in separate groups, all are conquered. The climate is wretched, with its frequent rains and mists, but there is no extreme cold. Their day is longer than in our part of the world. The nights are light, and in the extreme north so short that evening and morning twilight are scarcely distinguishable. If no clouds block the view, the sun's glow, it is said, can be seen all night long: it does not set and rise, but simply passes along the horizon. The reason must be that the flat extremities of the earth cast low shadows and do not raise the darkness to any height; night therefore fails to reach the sky and its stars. The soil will produce good crops, except olives, vines, and other plants which usually grow in warmer lands. They are slow to ripen, though they shoot up quickly – both facts being due to the same cause, the extreme moistness of the soil and atmosphere. Britain yields gold, silver, and other metals, to make it worth conquering. Its seas, too, produce pearls, but they are of a dark, bluish-grey colour. Some think that the natives are unskilful in gathering them; for whereas in the Indian Ocean the oysters are torn alive and breathing from the rocks, in Britain they are collected as the sea throws them up. I find it easier to believe that the pearls are of inferior quality than that people miss a chance of making a larger profit.

13

The Britons readily submit to military service, payment of tribute, and other obligations imposed by government, provided that there is no abuse. That they bitterly resent; for they are broken in to obedience, but not as yet to slavery. Julius Caesar, the first Roman to enter Britain with an army, did indeed intimidate the natives by a victory and secure a grip on the coast. But he may fairly be said to have merely drawn attention to the island: it was not his to bequeath. After him came the civil wars, with the leading men of Rome fighting against their country. Even when peace returned, Britain was long neglected. Augustus spoke of this as 'policy', Tiberius called it an 'injunction'. The emperor Gaius unquestionably planned an invasion of Britain; but his impulsive ideas shifted like a weathercock, and his grandiose efforts against Germany had come to nothing. It was the late emperor Claudius who initiated the great undertaking. He sent over legions and auxiliaries and chose Vespasian to share in the enterprise – the first step towards his future greatness. Tribes were subdued and kings captured, and the finger of destiny began to point to Vespasian.

14

The first governor of consular rank to be appointed was Aulus Plautius, and soon after him came Ostorius Scapula – both of them fine soldiers. Not only were the nearest parts of Britain gradually organized into a province, but a colony of veterans also was founded. Certain domains were presented to King Cogidumnus, who maintained his unswerving loyalty right down to our own times – an example of the long-established Roman custom of employing even kings to make others slaves. Didius Gallus, the next governor, merely held what his predecessors had won, establishing a few forts in more advanced positions, so that he could claim the credit of having made some annexations. Veranius succeeded Didius, only to die within the year. After him, Suetonius Paulinus enjoyed two years of success, conquering fresh tribes and strengthening forts. Emboldened thereby to attack the island of Anglesey, which was feeding the native resistance, he exposed himself to attack in the rear.

15

For the Britons, their fears allayed by the absence of the dreaded legate, began to canvass the woes of slavery, to compare their wrongs and sharpen their sting in the telling. 'We gain nothing by submission except heavier burdens for willing shoulders. We used to have one king at a time; now two are set over us – the governor to wreak his fury on our life-blood; the procurator, on our property. Whether our masters quarrel with each other or agree together, our bondage is equally ruinous. The governor has centurions to execute his will; the procurator, slaves; and both of them add insults to violence. Nothing is any longer safe from their greed and lust. In war it is at least a braver man who takes the spoil; as things stand with us, it is mostly cowards and shirkers that seize our homes, kidnap our children, and conscript our men – as though it were only for our own country that we would not face death. What a mere handful our invaders are, if we reckon up our own numbers! Such thoughts prompted the Germans to throw off the yoke; and they have only a river, not the Ocean, to shield them. We have country, wives, and parents to fight for; the Romans have nothing but greed and self-indulgence. Back they will go, as their deified Julius went back, if we will but emulate the valour of our fathers. We must not be scared by the loss of one or two battles; success may give an army more dash, but the greater staying-power comes from defeat. The gods themselves are at last showing mercy to us Britons in keeping the Roman general away, with his army exiled in another island. For ourselves, we have already taken the most difficult step: we have begun to plan. And in an enterprise like this there is more danger in being caught planning than in taking the plunge.'

16

Egged on by such mutual encouragements, the whole island rose under the leadership of Boudicca, a lady of royal descent – for Britons make no distinction of sex in their appointment of commanders. They hunted down the Roman troops in their scattered posts, stormed the forts, and assaulted the colony itself, which they saw as the citadel of their servitude; and there was no form of savage cruelty that the angry victors refrained from. In fact, had not Paulinus, on hearing of the revolt, made speed to help, Britain would have been lost. As it was, he restored it to its former state of submission by a single successful action. But many of the rebels did not lay down their arms, conscious of their guilt and of the special reasons they had for dreading what the governor might do. Excellent officer though he was, it was feared that he would abuse their surrender and punish every offence with undue severity, as if it were a personal injury. The government therefore replaced him by Petronius Turpilianus. They hoped that he would be more inclined to listen to pleas in extenuation of guilt or protestations of repentance, since he had not witnessed the enemy's crimes. He dealt with the existing troubles, but risked no further move before handing over his post to Trebellius Maximus. Trebellius was deficient in energy and without military experience, but he kept control of the province by an easy-going kind of administration. The barbarians now learned, like any Romans, to condone seductive vices, while the intervention of the civil wars provided him with a valid excuse for inactivity. There was, however, a serious mutiny; for the troops, accustomed to campaigns, got out of hand when they had nothing to do. Trebellius fled and hid to escape his angry army. His honour and dignity compromised, he now commanded merely on sufferance. By a kind of tacit bargain the troops had licence to do as they pleased, the general had his life; and so the mutiny stopped short of bloodshed. Vettius Bolanus likewise, as the civil wars still continued, declined to disturb the province by enforcing discipline. There was still the same paralysis in face of the foe, the same insubordination in the camp – only Bolanus was an upright man, with no misdeeds to make him hated, and had won affection where he lacked authority.

17

But when Vespasian, in the course of his general triumph,
restored stable government to Britain, there came a
succession of great generals and splendid armies, and the
hopes of our enemies dwindled. Petilius Cerealis at once
struck terror into their hearts by attacking the state of the
Brigantes, which is said to be the most populous in the
whole province. After a series of battles – some of them
by no means bloodless – Petilius had overrun, if not
actually conquered, the major part of their territory. He
would indeed have completely eclipsed the record and
reputation of any ordinary successor. But Julius Frontinus
was equal to shouldering the heavy burden, and rose as
high as a man then could rise. He subdued by force of arms
the strong and warlike nation of the Silures, after a hard
struggle, not only against the valour of his enemy, but
against the difficulties of the terrain.

18

Such was the condition to which Britain had been
brought by the ups and downs of warfare when Agricola
crossed the Channel with the summer already half over.
The soldiers thought they had done with campaigning
for the present and were relaxing, while the enemy were
looking for a chance to profit thereby. Shortly before his
arrival the tribe of the Ordovices had almost wiped out a
squadron of cavalry stationed in their territory, and this

initial stroke had excited the province. Those who wanted war welcomed the lead thus given, and only waited to test the temper of the new governor. The summer was now far spent, the auxiliary units were scattered all over the province, and the soldiers assumed that there would be no more fighting that year. Everything, in fact, combined to hinder or delay a new campaign, and many were in favour of simply watching the points where danger threatened. In spite of all, Agricola decided to go and meet the peril. He concentrated the legionaries serving on detachment duties and a small force of auxiliaries. As the Ordovices did not venture to descend into the plain, he led his men up into the hills, marching in front himself so as to impart his own courage to the rest by sharing their danger, and cut to pieces almost the whole fighting force of the tribe. But he realized that he must continue to live up to his reputation, and that the outcome of his first enterprises would determine how much fear his subsequent operations would inspire. So he decided to reduce the island of Anglesey, from the occupation of which Paulinus had been recalled by the revolt of all Britain, as I described in an earlier chapter. As the plan was hastily conceived, there was no fleet at hand; but Agricola's resource and resolution found means of getting troops across. He carefully picked out from his auxiliaries men who had experience of shallow waters and had been trained at home to swim carrying their arms and keeping their horses under control, and made them discard all their equipment. He then launched them on a surprise attack; and the enemy, who had been thinking in terms of a fleet of ships and naval operations, were completely nonplussed. What could embarrass or defeat a foe who attacked like that? So they sued for peace and surrendered the island; and Agricola was extolled as a brilliant governor, who immediately on his arrival – a time usually devoted to pageantry and a round of ceremonial visits – had chosen to undertake an arduous and dangerous enterprise. Yet he did not use his success to glorify himself. He would not represent his action as a campaign of conquest, when, as he said, he had merely kept a defeated tribe under control. He did not even use laurel-wreathed dispatches to announce his achievement. But his very reluctance to admit his title to fame won him even greater fame: for men gauged his splendid hopes for the future by his reticence about an exploit so remarkable.

19

Agricola, however, understood the feelings of the province and had learned from the experience of others that arms can effect little if injustice follows in their train. He resolved to root out the causes of rebellion. Beginning with himself and his staff, he enforced discipline in his own establishment first – a task often found as difficult as the government of a province. He made no use of freedmen or slaves for official business. He would not be influenced by his personal preference, or by recommendations or petitions, in choosing centurions and men for staff duties. The best, he was sure, would best justify his trust. He knew everything that went on, but did not always act upon his knowledge. He would condone minor offences, but dealt severely with major crimes. However, he did not always pronounce sentence: if an offender was truly repentant, more often than not he was content with that. He preferred to appoint to official positions and duties men whom he could trust not to transgress, rather than have to punish transgressions. He made the contributions of corn and tribute less onerous by distributing the burdens fairly, and put a stop to the tricks of profiteers, which were more bitterly resented than the tax itself. For the provincials were made to wait outside locked granaries in order to go through the farce of 'buying' corn to deliver to the governor – thus being in fact compelled to discharge their obligations by money payments. Or delivery would be ordered to out-of-the-way destinations at the other end of the country, so that states which had permanent camps close by them were told to send supplies to remote and inaccessible spots. Thus the rendering of a service which should have been easy for all was obstructed in order to line a few men's pockets.

20

By checking these abuses in his very first year of office Agricola made the Britons appreciate the advantages of peace, which, through the negligence or arbitrariness of previous governors, had been as much feared as war.

But when summer came he concentrated his army and took the field in person. He was present everywhere on the march, praising good discipline and keeping stragglers up to the mark. He himself chose sites for camps and reconnoitred estuaries and forests; and all the time he gave the enemy no rest, but constantly launched plundering raids. Then, when he had done enough to inspire fear, he tried the effect of clemency and showed them the attractions of peace. As a result, many states which till then had maintained their independence gave hostages and abandoned their resentful attitude. A ring of garrisoned forts was placed round them; and so skilfully and thoroughly was the operation carried through that no British tribes ever made their first submission with so little interference from their neighbours.

21

The following winter was spent on schemes of social betterment. Agricola had to deal with people living in isolation and ignorance, and therefore prone to fight; and his object was to accustom them to a life of peace and quiet by the provision of amenities. He therefore gave private encouragement and official assistance to the building of temples, public squares, and good houses. He praised the energetic and scolded the slack; and competition for honour proved as effective as compulsion. Furthermore, he educated the sons of the chiefs in the liberal arts, and expressed a preference for British ability as compared with the trained skills of the Gauls. The result was that instead of loathing the Latin language they became eager to speak it effectively. In the same way, our national dress came into favour and the toga was everywhere to be seen. And so the population was gradually led into the demoralizing temptations of arcades, baths, and sumptuous banquets. The unsuspecting Britons spoke of such novelties as 'civilization', when in fact they were only a feature of their enslavement.

22

The third year of Agricola's campaigns brought him into contact with fresh peoples; for the territory of tribes was ravaged as far north as the estuary called the Tay. Our army was buffeted by furious storms, but the enemy were now too terrified to molest it. There was even time to spare for the establishment of forts. It has been observed by experts that no general ever showed a better eye for ground than Agricola. No fort on a site of his choosing was ever taken by storm, ever capitulated, or was ever abandoned. On the contrary, the garrisons could frequently venture upon sallies; for they were secured against protracted siege by having supplies sufficient for a whole year. And so winter in these forts held no terrors and every commandant could look after himself. The enemy were baffled and in despair. They could no longer retrieve the losses of the summer by successes in the winter, but were equally hard pressed at both seasons.

Agricola was not greedy of fame and never tried to steal

the credit for other men's work. Every centurion and prefect found in him an honest witness to his merit. According to some accounts he was harsh in reprimand; and certainly he could make himself as unpleasant to the wrong kind of man as he was agreeable to the right kind. But his anger left no hidden malice in his heart, and you had no need to fear his silence. He thought it more honourable to hurt than to hate.

23

The fourth summer was spent in securing the districts already overrun; and if the valour of our army and the glory of Rome had permitted such a thing, a good place for halting the advance was found in Britain itself. The Clyde and the Forth, carried inland to a great depth on the tides of opposite seas, are separated only by a narrow neck of land. This isthmus was now firmly held by garrisons, and the whole expanse of country to the south was safely in our hands. The enemy had been pushed into what was virtually another island.

24

Agricola started his fifth campaign by crossing the river Annan, and in a series of successful actions subdued nations hitherto unknown. The side of Britain that faces Ireland was lined with his forces. His motive was rather hope than fear. Ireland, lying between Britain and Spain, and easily accessible also from the Gallic sea, might serve as a very valuable link between the provinces forming the strongest part of the empire. It is small in comparison with Britain, but larger than the islands of the Mediterranean. In soil and climate, and in the character and civilization of its inhabitants, it is much like Britain; and its approaches and harbours have now become better known from merchants who trade there. An Irish prince, expelled from his home by a rebellion, was welcomed by Agricola, who detained him, nominally as a friend, in the hope of being able to make use of him. I have often heard Agricola say that Ireland could be reduced and held by a single legion with a fair-sized force of auxiliaries; and that it would be easier to hold Britain if it were completely surrounded by Roman armies, so that liberty was banished from its sight.

25

In the summer in which his sixth year of office began, Agricola enveloped the tribes beyond the Forth. Fearing a general rising of the northern nations and threatening movements by the enemy on land, he used his fleet to reconnoitre the harbours. It was first employed by Agricola to increase his striking-power, and its continued attendance on him made an excellent impression. The war was pushed forward simultaneously by land and sea; and infantry, cavalry, and marines, often meeting in the same camp, would mess and make merry together. They boasted, as soldiers will, of their several exploits and adventures, and matched the perilous depths of woods and ravines against the hazards of storms and waves, victories on land against the conquest of the ocean. The Britons for their part, as was learned from prisoners, were dismayed by the appearance of the fleet; now that the secret places of their sea were opened up, they felt that their last refuge in defeat was closed against them. The natives of Caledonia turned to armed resistance on a large scale – though the facts were exaggerated, as the unknown always is, by rumour. They went so far as to attack some of our forts, and inspired alarm by their challenging offensive. There were cowards in the council who pleaded for a 'strategic retreat' behind the Forth, maintaining that 'evacuation was preferable to expulsion'. But just then Agricola learned that the enemy was about to attack in several columns. For fear that their superior numbers and knowledge of the country might enable them to surround him, he moved his own army forward in three divisions.

26

As soon as the enemy got to know of this they suddenly changed their plans and massed for a night attack on the ninth legion. That seemed to them the weakest point. Striking panic into the sleeping camp, they cut down the sentries and broke in. The fight was already raging inside the camp when Agricola was warned by his scouts of the enemy's march. He followed close on their tracks, ordered the speediest of his cavalry and infantry to harass the assailants' rear, and finally made his whole force raise a shout. Dawn was now breaking, and the gleam of the legions' standards could be seen. Caught thus between two fires, the Britons were dismayed, while the men of the ninth took heart again; now that their lives were safe they could fight for honour. They even made a sally, and a grim struggle ensued in the narrow gateways. At last the enemy were routed by the efforts of the two armies – the one striving to make it plain that they had brought relief; the other, that they could have done without it. Had not marshes and woods covered the enemy's retreat, that victory would have ended the war.

27

This success inspired with confidence all the troops who had taken part in it or heard about it. They declared that nothing could stop men like them, that they ought to drive deeper into Caledonia and fight battle after battle till they reached the farthest limits of Britain. Even the cautious strategists of yesterday were forward and boastful enough after the event. That is the crowning injustice of war: all claim credit for success, while defeat is laid to the account of one. The Britons, on their part, felt that they had not lost through any lack of courage, but through the Roman general's skilful use of a lucky chance. With unbroken spirit they persisted in arming their whole fighting force, putting their wives and children in places of safety, and assembling together to ratify their league by sacrificial rites. Thus the campaign ended with angry feelings excited on both sides.

28

That same summer a cohort of the Usipi that had been enrolled in Germany and transferred to Britain ventured upon a memorable exploit. They murdered a centurion and some soldiers who, to teach them discipline, were serving in their ranks as models and instructors. Then they boarded three small warships, forcing the pilots to do their will; but one of these escaped and went back, and the other two were then looked on with such suspicion that they were killed. News of these events had not yet got about, and the ships seemed like a ghostly apparition as they coasted along. But the time came when they had to put in to land to get water and other supplies. This brought them into collision with parties of Britons who tried to protect their property. Though often successful, the raiders were sometimes driven off; and in the end they were so near starvation that they began to eat one another; first they picked out the weakest, then they drew lots. In this fashion they sailed round North Britain; then they lost their ships through bad seamanship, were taken for pirates, and were cut off first by the Suebi and then by the Frisii. Some of them were sold as slaves and passed from hand to hand till they reached our bank of the Rhine, where they gained notoriety by telling the story of their wonderful adventure.

29

At the beginning of the next summer Agricola suffered a grievous personal loss in the death of a son who had been born a year before. He accepted this blow without either parading the fortitude of a stoic or giving way to passionate grief like a woman. The conduct of the war was one means he used to distract his mind from its sorrow. He sent his fleet ahead to plunder at various points and thus spread uncertainty and terror; then, with an army marching light, which he had reinforced with some of the bravest of the Britons who had proved their loyalty by long years of submission, he reached Mount Graupius, which he found occupied by the enemy. The Britons were, in fact, undaunted by the loss of the previous battle, and were ready for either revenge or enslavement. They had realized at last that the common danger must be warded off by united action, and had sent round embassies and drawn up treaties to rally the full force of all their states. Already more than 30,000 men could be seen, and still they came flocking to the colours – all the young men, and famous warriors whose 'old age was fresh and green', every man wearing the decorations he had earned. At that point one of the many leaders, a man of outstanding valour and nobility named Calgacus, addressed the close-packed multitude of men clamouring for battle. This is the substance of what he is reported to have said:

30

'When I consider the motives we have for fighting and the critical position we are in, I have a strong feeling that the united front you are showing today will mean the dawn of liberty for the whole of Britain. You have mustered to a man, and all of you are free. There are no lands behind us, and even on the sea we are menaced by the Roman fleet. The clash of battle – the hero's glory – has now actually become the safest refuge for a coward. Battles against Rome have been lost and won before; but hope was never abandoned, since we were always here in reserve. We, the choicest flower of Britain's manhood, were hidden away in her most secret places. Out of sight of subject shores, we kept even our eyes free from the defilement of tyranny. We, the most distant dwellers upon earth, the last of the free, have been shielded till today by our very remoteness and by the obscurity in which it has shrouded our name. Now, the farthest bounds of Britain lie open to our enemies; and what men know nothing about they always assume to be a valuable prize. But there are no more nations beyond us; nothing is there but waves and rocks, and the Romans, more deadly still than these – for in them is an arrogance which no submission or good behaviour can escape. Pillagers of the world, they have exhausted the land by their indiscriminate plunder, and now they ransack the sea. A rich enemy excites their cupidity; a poor one, their lust for power. East and West alike have failed to satisfy them. They are the only people on earth to whose covetousness both riches and poverty are equally tempting. To robbery, butchery, and rapine, they give the lying name of "government"; they create a desolation and call it peace.

31

'Nature has ordained that every man should love his children and his other relatives above all else. These are now being torn from us by conscription to slave in other lands. Our wives and sisters, even if they are not raped by enemy soldiers, are seduced by men who are supposed to be our friends and guests. Our goods and money are consumed by taxation; our land is stripped of its harvest to fill their granaries; our hands and limbs are crippled by building roads through forests and swamps under the lash of our oppressors. Creatures born to be slaves are sold once for all, and, what is more, get their keep from their owners. We Britons are sold into slavery anew every day; we have to pay the purchase-price ourselves and feed our masters into the bargain. In a private household the latest arrival is made the butt even of his fellow-slaves; so, in this establishment where all mankind have long been slaves, it is we, the cheap new acquisitions, who are marked out for destruction. For we have no fertile lands, no mines, no ports, which we might be spared to work in. Our courage, too, and our martial spirit are against us: masters do not like such qualities in their subjects. Even our remoteness and isolation, while they give us protection, are bound to make the Romans wonder what mischief we are up to. Since you cannot hope for mercy, therefore, take courage before it is too late to strive for what you hold most dear, whether it be life or honour. The Brigantes, with only a woman to lead them, burned a Roman colony and stormed a camp; and if success had not tempted them to relax their efforts, they might have cast off the yoke. We, who have never been forced to feel that yoke, shall be fighting to preserve our freedom, and not, like them, merely to avenge past injuries. Let us then show, at the very first clash of arms, what manner of men Caledonia has kept in reserve.

32

'Do you imagine that the Romans' bravery in war matches their dissoluteness in time of peace? No! It is our quarrels and disunion that have given them fame. The reputation of the Roman army is built up on the faults of its enemies. Look at it, a motley conglomeration of nations, that will be shattered by defeat as surely as it is now held together by success. Or can you seriously think that those Gauls and Germans – and, to our bitter shame, many Britons too – are bound to Rome by genuine loyalty or affection? They may be lending their life-blood now to the foreign tyrant, but they were enemies of Rome for more years than they have been her slaves. Terror and intimidation are poor bonds of attachment: once break them, and where fear ends hatred will begin. All that can spur men on to victory is on our side. The enemy have no wives to fire their courage, no parents ready to taunt them if they run away. Most of them either have no fatherland they can remember, or belong to one other than Rome. See them, a scanty band, scared and bewildered, staring blankly at the unfamiliar sky, sea, and forests around them. The gods have given them, like so many prisoners bound hand and foot, into our hands. Be not afraid of the outward show that means nothing, the glitter of gold and silver that can neither avert nor inflict a wound. Even in the ranks of our enemies we shall find willing hands to help us. The Britons will recognize our cause as their own; the Gauls will remember their lost liberty; the rest of the Germans will desert them as surely as the Usipi did recently. And beyond this army that you see there is nothing to be frightened of – only forts without garrisons, colonies of greybeards, towns sick and distracted between rebel subjects and tyrant masters. Which will you choose – to follow your leader into battle, or to submit to taxation, labour in the mines, and all the other tribulations of slavery? Whether you are to endure these for ever or take quick vengeance, this field must decide. On, then, into action; and as you go, think of those that went before you and of those that shall come after.'

33

This speech was received with enthusiasm, expressed, in barbarian fashion, by singing and yelling and by discordant cries. Bodies of troops began to move and arms flashed as the most adventurous ran out in front, and all the time their battle-line was taking shape. Agricola's soldiers were in such high spirits that they could scarcely be kept within their defences. For all that, he felt it desirable to put the final edge on their courage, and addressed them thus:

'This is the seventh year, comrades, since by loyal service – yours and my own – you started to conquer Britain in the name of imperial Rome's divinely guided greatness. In all these campaigns and battles, which have called not only for courage in face of the enemy but for toil and endurance in fighting, as it were, against Nature herself, I have had no complaint to make of my men nor you of your general. Thus we have advanced beyond the limits reached by previous armies under my predecessors. The farthest boundary of this land, which they knew only by report or rumour, we hold in our grasp with arms and fortresses. We have both explored and conquered Britain. Many a time on the march, as you trudged wearily over marshes, mountains, and rivers, have I heard the bravest among you exclaim: "When shall we meet the enemy? When will they come and fight us?" They are coming now, for we have dug them out of their hiding-places. The fair field for our valour that we desired is granted to us. An easy path awaits us if we win, but if we lose the going will be hard indeed. The long road that we have travelled, the forests we have threaded our way through, the estuaries we have crossed

– all redound to our credit and honour as long as we keep our eyes to the front. But if we turn tail, our success in surmounting these obstacles will put us in the deadliest peril. We have not the exact knowledge of the country that our enemy has, or his abundant supplies. However, we have our hands, and swords in them, and these are all that matters. For myself, I made up my mind long ago that neither an army nor a commander can avoid danger by running away. So – although an honourable death would be better than a disgraceful attempt to save our lives – our best chance of safety does in fact lie in doing our duty. And there would be glory, too, in dying – if die we must – here where the world and all created things come to an end.

34

'If you were confronted by strange nations and unfamiliar troops, I would quote the examples of other armies to encourage you. As things are, you need only recall your own battle-honours, only question your own eyes. These are the men who last year attacked a single legion like robbers in the night, and acknowledged defeat when they heard your battle-cry. These are the greatest runaways of all the Britons – which is the reason why they have survived so long. When we plunged into woods and gorges on the march, all the brave beasts used to charge straight at us, while the timid and slothful ones slunk away at the mere sound of our tread. It is the same now. The most courageous of the Britons have fallen long since; those who remain are just so many spiritless cowards. You have overtaken them at last, not because they have chosen to stand at bay, but because they are cornered. It is only their desperate plight and deadly fear that have paralysed their army where it stands, for you to win a great and brilliant victory over it. Have done with campaigning; crown fifty years with one glorious day, and prove to Rome that her soldiers were never to blame if wars have been allowed to drag on or the seeds of fresh rebellion sown.'

35

Even while Agricola was still speaking the troops showed intense eagerness, and the end of his speech was greeted with a wild burst of enthusiasm. Without delay they went off to arm themselves. The men were so thrilled that they were ready to rush straight into action; but Agricola marshalled them with care. The auxiliary infantry, 8,000 in number, formed a strong centre, while 3,000 cavalry were distributed on the flanks. The legions were stationed in front of the camp rampart: victory would be vastly more glorious if it cost no Roman blood, while if the auxiliaries should be repulsed the legions could come to their rescue. The British army was posted on higher ground in a manner calculated to impress and intimidate its enemy. Their front line was on the plain, but the other ranks seemed to mount up the sloping hillside in close-packed tiers. The flat space between the two armies was taken up by the noisy manoeuvring of the charioteers.

Agricola now saw that he was greatly outnumbered, and fearing that the enemy might fall simultaneously on his front and flanks, he opened out his ranks. The line now looked like being dangerously thin, and many urged him to bring up the legions. But he was always an optimist and resolute in the face of difficulties. He sent away his horse and took up his position on foot in front of the colours.

36

The fighting began with exchanges of missiles, and the Britons showed both steadiness and skill in parrying our spears with their huge swords or catching them on their little shields, while they themselves rained volleys on us. At last Agricola called upon four cohorts of Batavians and two of Tungrians to close and fight it out at the sword's point. These old soldiers had been well drilled in sword-fighting, while the enemy were awkward at it, with their small shields and unwieldy swords, especially as the latter, having no points, were quite unsuitable for a cut-and-thrust struggle at close quarters. The Batavians, raining blow after blow, striking them with the bosses of their shields, and stabbing them in the face, felled the Britons posted on the plain and pushed on up the hill-sides. This provoked the other cohorts to attack with vigour and kill the nearest of the enemy. Many Britons were left behind half dead or even unwounded, owing to the very speed of our victory. Our cavalry squadrons, meanwhile, had routed the war chariots, and now plunged into the infantry battle. Their first onslaught was terrifying, but the solid ranks of the enemy and the roughness of the ground soon brought them to a standstill and made the battle quite unlike a cavalry action. Our infantry had only a precarious foothold and were being jostled by the horses' flanks; and often a runaway chariot, or riderless horses careering about wildly in their terror, came plunging into the ranks from the side or in head-on collision.

37

The Britons on the hill-tops had so far taken no part in the action and had leisure to note with contempt the smallness of our numbers. They were now starting to descend gradually and envelop our victorious rear. But Agricola, who had expected just such a move, threw in their path four squadrons of cavalry which he was keeping in hand for emergencies and turned their spirited charge into a disorderly rout. The tactics of the Britons now recoiled on themselves. Our squadrons, obedient to orders, rode round from the front of the battle and fell upon the enemy in the rear. The open plain now presented a grim, awe-inspiring spectacle. Our horsemen kept pursuing them, wounding some, making prisoners of others, and then killing them as new enemies appeared. On the British side, each man now behaved according to his character. Whole groups, though they had weapons in their hands, fled before inferior numbers; elsewhere, unarmed men deliberately charged to face certain death.

Equipment, bodies, and mangled limbs lay all around on the bloodstained earth; and even the vanquished now and then recovered their fury and their courage. When they reached the woods, they rallied and profited by their local knowledge to ambush the first rash pursuers. Our men's over-confidence might even have led to serious disaster. But Agricola was everywhere at once. He ordered strong cohorts of light infantry to ring the woods like hunters. Where the thickets were denser, dismounted troopers went in to scour them; where they thinned out, the cavalry did the work. At length, when they saw our troops, re-formed and steady, renewing the pursuit, the Britons turned and ran. They no longer kept formation or looked to see where their comrades were, but scattering and deliberately keeping apart from each other they penetrated far into trackless wilds. The pursuit went on till night fell and our soldiers were tired of killing. Of the enemy some 10,000 fell; on our side, 360 men – among them Aulus Atticus, the prefect of a cohort, whose youthful impetuosity and mettlesome horse carried him deep into the ranks of the enemy.

38

For the victors it was a night of rejoicing over their triumph and their booty. The Britons dispersed, men and women wailing together, as they carried away their wounded or called to the survivors. Many left their homes and in their rage actually set fire to them, or chose hiding-places, only to abandon them at once. At one moment they would try to concert plans, then suddenly break off their conference. Sometimes the sight of their dear ones broke their hearts; more often it goaded them to fury; and we had proof that some of them laid violent hands on their wives and children in a kind of pity. The next day revealed the effects of our victory more fully. An awful silence reigned on every hand; the hills were deserted, houses smoking in the distance, and our scouts did not meet a soul. These were sent out in all directions and made sure that the enemy had fled at random and were not massing at any point. As the summer was almost over, it was impossible for operations to be extended over a wider area; so Agricola led his army into the territory of the Boresti. There he took hostages and ordered his admiral to sail round the north of Britain. A detachment of troops was assigned to him, and the terror of Rome had gone before him. Agricola himself, marching slowly in order to overawe the recently conquered tribes by the very deliberateness of his movements, placed his infantry and cavalry in winter-quarters. At about the same time the fleet, which aided by favourable weather had completed a remarkable voyage, reached Trucculensis Portus. It had started the voyage from that harbour, and after coasting along the adjacent shore of Britain had returned intact.

39

Agricola's dispatch reported this series of events in language of careful moderation. But Domitian reacted as he often did: he pretended to be pleased when in fact he was deeply disturbed. He was conscious of the ridicule that his sham triumph over Germany had excited, when he had bought slaves in the market to have their dress and hair made up to look like prisoners of war. But now came a genuine victory on the grand scale: the enemy dead were reckoned in thousands, and the popular acclaim was immense. He knew that there was nothing so dangerous for him as to have the name of a subject exalted above that of the emperor. He had only wasted his time in silencing forensic eloquence and suppressing all outstanding accomplishment in civil life, if another man was to snatch military glory from his grasp. Talents in other directions could at a pinch be ignored; but the qualities of a good general should be the monopoly of the emperor. Harassed by these anxieties, he brooded over them in secret till he was tired – a sure sign in him of some malevolent purpose. In the end he decided that it would be best to store up his hatred for the present and wait for the first burst of popular applause and the enthusiasm of the army to die down. For at that time Agricola was still in command of Britain.

40

Domitian therefore directed that the customary decorations of a triumph, the honour of a complimentary statue, and all the other substitutes for a triumphal procession, should be voted to Agricola in the Senate, coupled with a highly flattering address; further, the impression was to be conveyed that the province of Syria, then vacant through the death of Atilius Rufus, an ex-consul, and always reserved for men of seniority, was intended for Agricola. It was commonly believed that one of the freedmen in Domitian's closest confidence was sent with a letter offering Syria to Agricola, but with orders to deliver it only if he was still in Britain. The freedman, it is said, met Agricola's ship in the Channel, and without even seeking an interview with him returned to Domitian. The story may be true, or it may have been invented as being characteristic of Domitian. Agricola, meanwhile, had handed over the province to his successor in a state of peace and security. To avoid publicity, he did not want to be met by a crowd of people when he returned to Rome. So he evaded the attentions of his friends and entered the city by night. By night, too, he went, in accordance with instructions, to the palace. He was greeted with a perfunctory kiss and then dismissed, without a word of conversation, to join the crowd of courtiers dancing attendance on the emperor. Wishing to divert attention from his military repute, which was apt to offend civilians, by displaying other qualities, Agricola devoted himself completely to a life of quiet retirement. He was modest in his manner of life, courteous in conversation, and never seen with more than one or two friends. Consequently, the majority who always measure great men by their self-advertisement, after carefully observing Agricola, were left asking why he was so famous. Very few could read his secret aright.

41

Often during this period Agricola was denounced to Domitian behind his back, and acquitted behind his back. His danger did not arise from any charge against him or any complaint from a victim of injustice, but from the emperor's hatred of merit, Agricola's own fame, and that deadliest type of enemy, the singers of his praises. And indeed the fortunes of Rome in those ensuing years were such as would not allow Agricola's name to be forgotten. One after another, armies were lost in Moesia and Dacia, in Germany and Pannonia, through the rash folly or cowardice of their generals; one after another, experienced officers were defeated in fortified positions and captured with all their troops. It was no longer the frontier and the Danube line that were threatened, but the permanent quarters of the legions and the maintenance of the empire. So, as one loss followed another and year after year was signalized by death and disaster, public opinion began to clamour for Agricola to take command. His energy and resolution, and his proven courage in war, were universally contrasted with the general slackness and cowardice. It is known that Domitian's own ears were stung by the lash of such talk. The best of his freedmen spoke out of their loyal affection, the worst out of malice and spleen; but all alike goaded on an emperor who was always inclined to pursue evil courses. And so Agricola, by his own virtues and by the faults of others, was carried straight along the perilous path that led to glory.

42

At length the year arrived in which he was due to ballot for the proconsulship of Africa or Asia; and the recent execution of Civica was both a warning for Agricola and a precedent for Domitian. Agricola was approached by some of the emperor's confidants, who had been instructed to ask him outright whether he meant to take a province. They began by hinting at the attractions of peaceful retirement, went on to offer their help in getting his excuses accepted if he wished to decline, and finally, throwing off the mask, prevailed on him by persuasions and threats to go to Domitian. The emperor had his hypocrite's part prepared. He put on a majestic air, listened to Agricola's request to be excused, and after granting it allowed Agricola to thank him, without even a blush for such an odious pretence of granting a favour. He did not, however, assign him the usual proconsular salary, which he himself had granted in some cases – perhaps from annoyance that Agricola had not asked for it, perhaps from an uneasy conscience, not wishing people to think he had bribed him to decline when in fact he had forbidden him to accept. It is an instinct of human nature to hate a man whom you have injured. Yet even Domitian, though he was quick to anger, and his resentment all the more implacable because he generally tried to hide it, was softened by the self-restraint and wisdom of Agricola, who declined to court, by a defiant and futile parade of independence, the renown that must inevitably destroy him. Let it be clear to those who insist on admiring disobedience that even under bad emperors men can be great, and that a decent regard for authority, if backed by industry and energy, can reach that peak of distinction which most men attain only by following a perilous course, winning fame, without benefiting their country, by an ostentatious self-martyrdom.

43

The end of Agricola's life – a grievous blow to us and a sorrow to his friends – affected even men outside his own circle and complete strangers. The general public, usually so absorbed in their own concerns, flocked to his house to make enquiries; and in the public squares, and wherever people met for conversation, he was talked of. When his death was announced, no one was glad and no one quickly forgot him. Sympathy was increased by a persistent rumour that he had been poisoned. For my own part, I would not venture to assert that there is any positive evidence. However, throughout his illness there were more visits from prominent freedmen and court physicians than is usual with emperors when paying calls by proxy. This could have indicated genuine concern, or it may have been spying. All accounts agreed that on the last day, as he lay dying, every change in his condition was reported by relays of couriers, and no one could believe that tidings need have been brought so quickly if they were unwelcome to the emperor. However, Domitian made a decent show of sorrow; his hatred of Agricola no longer made him uneasy, and he could always hide satisfaction more convincingly than fear. It was no secret that on the reading of Agricola's will, which named Domitian as co-heir with his 'good wife' and his 'loving daughter', the Emperor was much pleased, taking it as a sincere compliment. His mind was so blinded and vitiated by incessant flattery that he did not realize that no good father would leave property to any emperor except a bad one.

44

Agricola was born on 13 June in the third consulship of the emperor Gaius and died in his fifty-fourth year on 23 August in the consulship of Collega and Priscinus. As to his personal appearance – in case the interest of posterity should extend to such a matter – he was good-looking rather than striking. His features did not indicate a passionate nature: the prevailing impression was one of charm. There was no difficulty about recognizing him as a good man, and one could willingly believe him to be a great man. Though he was taken from us in the prime of his vigorous manhood, yet, so far as glory is concerned, the longest span of years could not have made his life more complete. He had fully attained those true blessings which depend upon a man's own character. He had held the consulship and bore the decorations of triumph: what more could fortune have added? He had no desire for vast wealth, and he had a handsome fortune. He died while his wife and daughter yet lived to comfort him; and we may justly count him even fortunate who, with his honours unimpaired, at the height of his fame, leaving kinsmen and friends secure, escaped what was soon to come. Though he was not permitted to see the dawn of this blessed age and the principate of Trajan – a consummation of which he often spoke to us in wishful prophecy – yet it was no small compensation for his untimely cutting off that he was spared those last days when Domitian, instead of giving the state a breathing-space to recover from one blow before the next fell, rained them upon its head so thick and fast that its life-blood was drained as though by a single mortal wound.

45

Agricola did not live to see the senate-house under siege, the senators surrounded by a cordon of troops, and that one fell stroke which sent so many consulars to their death, so many noble ladies into banishment or exile. Only a single victory was credited as yet to Carus Mettius; the four walls of the Alban fortress still kept Messalinus's bellow from reaching our ears; and Massa Baebius was still a prisoner in the dock. But before long we senators led Helvidius to prison, watched in shame the sufferings of Mauricus and Rusticus, and stained ourselves with Senecio's innocent blood. Even Nero used to avert his eyes and, though he ordered abominations, forbore to witness them. The worst of our torments under Domitian was to see him with his eyes fixed upon us. Every sigh was registered against us; and when we all turned pale, he did not scruple to make us marked men by a glance of his savage countenance – that blood-red countenance which saved him from ever being seen to blush with shame.

Happy indeed were you, Agricola, not only in your glorious life, but in your timely death. We have the testimony of those who heard your last words that you met your fate with a cheerful courage. You seemed glad to do your best to acquit the emperor of blood-guiltiness. But your daughter and I have suffered more than the pang of a father's loss: we grieve that we could not sit by your sick-bed, sustain your failing strength, and satisfy our yearning for your fond looks and embraces. We should surely have received some last commands, some words to be engraved for ever on our hearts. It was our own special sorrow and pain that through the accident of our long absence we lost him four years before his death. All, more than all, dear father, was assuredly done to honour you by the devoted wife at your side. Yet some tears that should have been shed over you were not shed; and, at the last, there was something for which your dying eyes looked in vain.

46

If there is any mansion for the spirits of the just, if, as philosophers hold, great souls do not perish with the body, may you rest in peace! May you call us, your family, from feeble regrets and unmanly mourning to contemplate your virtues, for which it were a sin to mourn or lament! May we honour you in better ways – by our admiration and our praise, and if our powers permit by following your example! That is the true honour, the true affection of souls knit close to yours. To your daughter and widow I would suggest that they revere the memory of a father and a husband by continually pondering his deeds and sayings, and by treasuring in their hearts the form and features of his mind, rather than those of his body. Not that I would forbid likenesses of marble or of bronze. But representations of the human face, like that face itself, are subject to decay and dissolution, whereas the essence of man's mind is something everlasting, which you cannot preserve or express in material wrought by another's skill, but only in your own character. All that we loved and admired in Agricola abides and shall abide in the hearts of men through the endless procession of the ages; for his achievements are of great renown. With many it will be as with men who had no name or fame: they will be buried in oblivion. But Agricola's story is set on record for posterity, and he will live.

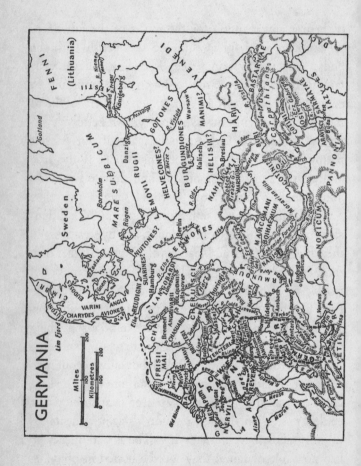

GERMANIA

1

THE various peoples of Germany are separated from the Gauls by the Rhine, from the Raetians and Pannonians by the Danube, and from the Sarmatians and Dacians by mountains – or, where there are no mountains, by mutual fear. The northern parts of the country are girdled by the sea, flowing round broad peninsulas and vast islands where a campaign of the present century has revealed to us the existence of some nations and kings hitherto unknown. The Rhine rises in a remote and precipitous height of the Raetian Alps and afterwards turns slightly westward to flow into the North Sea. The Danube issues from a gentle slope of moderate height in the Black Forest, and after passing more peoples than the Rhine in its course discharges itself into the Black Sea through six channels – a seventh mouth being lost in marshlands.

2

As to the Germans themselves, I think it probable that they are indigenous and that very little foreign blood has been introduced either by invasions or by friendly dealings with neighbouring peoples. For in former times it was not by land but on shipboard that would-be immigrants arrived; and the limitless ocean that lies beyond the coasts of Germany, and as it were defies intruders, is seldom visited by ships from our part of the world. And to say nothing of the perils of that wild and unknown sea, who would have been likely to leave Asia Minor, North Africa, or Italy, to go to Germany with its forbidding landscapes and unpleasant climate – a country that is thankless to till and dismal to behold for anyone who was not born and bred there?

In the traditional songs which form their only record of the past the Germans celebrate an earth-born god called Tuisto. His son Mannus is supposed to be the fountain-head of their race and himself to have begotten three sons who gave their names to three groups of tribes – the Ingaevones, nearest the sea; the Herminones, in the interior; and the Istaevones, who comprise all the rest. Some authorities, with the freedom of conjecture permitted by remote antiquity, assert that Tuisto had more numerous descendants and mention more tribal groups such as Marsi, Gambrivii, Suebi, and Vandilii – names which they affirm to be both genuine and ancient. The name *Germania*, however, is said to have been only recently applied to the country. The first people to cross the Rhine and appropriate Gallic territory, though they are known nowadays as Tungri, were at that time called *Germani*; and what was at first the name of this one tribe, not of the entire race, gradually came into general use in the wider sense. It was first applied to the whole people by the conquerors of the Gauls, to frighten them; later, all-the Germans adopted it and called themselves by the new name.

3

The Germans, like many other peoples, are said to have been visited by Hercules, and they sing of him as the foremost of all the heroes when they are about to engage in battle.* Ulysses also, in all those fabled wanderings of his, is supposed by some to have reached the northern sea and visited German lands, and to have founded and named Asciburgium, a town on the Rhine inhabited to this day. They even add that an altar consecrated by Ulysses and inscribed also with the name of his father Laertes was discovered long ago at this same place, and that certain barrows with monuments upon them bearing Greek inscriptions still exist on the borders of Germany and Raetia. I do not intend to argue either for or against these assertions; each man must accept or reject them as he feels inclined.

* They also have the well-known kind of chant that they call *baritus*. By the rendering of this they not only kindle their courage, but, merely by listening to the sound, they can forecast the issue of an approaching engagement. For they either terrify their foes or themselves become frightened, according to the character of the noise they make upon the battlefield; and they regard it not merely as so many voices chanting together but as a unison of valour. What they particularly aim at is a harsh, intermittent roar; and they hold their shields in front of their mouths, so that the sound is amplified iuto a deeper crescendo by the reverberation.

4

For myself, I accept the view that the peoples of Germany have never contaminated themselves by intermarriage with foreigners but remain of pure blood, distinct and unlike any other nation. One result of this is that their physical characteristics, in so far as one can generalize about such a large population, are always the same: fierce-looking blue eyes, reddish hair, and big frames – which, however, can exert their strength only by means of violent effort. They are less able to endure toil or fatiguing tasks and cannot bear thirst or heat, though their climate has inured them to cold spells and the poverty of their soil to hunger.

5

The appearance of the country differs considerably in different parts; but in general it is covered either by bristling forests or by foul swamps. It is wetter on the side that faces Gaul, windier on the side of Noricum and Pannonia. A good soil for cereal crops, it will not grow fruit-trees. It is well provided with live-stock; but the animals are mostly undersized, and even the cattle lack the handsome heads that are their natural glory. It is the mere number of them that the Germans take pride in; for these are the only form of wealth they have, and are much prized. Silver and gold have been denied them –

whether as a sign of divine favour or of divine wrath, I cannot say. Yet I would not positively assert that there are no deposits of silver or gold in Germany, since no one has prospected for them. The natives take less pleasure than most people do in possessing and handling these metals; indeed, one can see in their houses silver vessels, which have been presented to chieftains or to ambassadors travelling abroad, put to the same everyday uses as earthenware. Those who live on the frontiers nearest us, however, do value gold and silver for their use in commerce, being quick to recognize and pick out certain of our coin-types.* They like old-fashioned coins because they have been long familiar with them – especially those which have notched edges and are stamped with representations of two-horse chariots. They also prefer silver to gold, not from any special liking for the metal, but because a quantity of silver coins is more convenient for buying ordinary cheap merchandise.

6

Even iron is not plentiful; this has been inferred from the sort of weapons they have. Only a few of them use swords or large lances: they carry spears – called *frameae* in their language – with short and narrow blades, but so sharp and easy to handle that they can be used, as required, either at close quarters or in long-range fighting. Their

* The tribes of the interior stick to the simpler and more ancient practice of barter.

horsemen are content with a shield and a spear; but the foot-soldiers also rain javelins on their foes: each of them carries several, and they hurl them to immense distances, being naked or lightly clad in short cloaks. There is nothing ostentatious about their equipment: only their shields are picked out in the colours of their choice. Few have breastplates, and only one here and there a helmet of metal or hide. Their horses are not remarkable for either beauty or speed, and are not trained to execute various evolutions as ours are; they ride them straight ahead, or with just a single wheel to the right, keeping their line so well that not a man falls behind the rest. Generally speaking, their strength lies in infantry rather than cavalry. So foot-soldiers accompany the cavalry into action, their speed of foot being such that they can easily keep up with the charging horsemen. The best men are chosen from the whole body of young warriors and placed with the cavalry in front of the main battle-line. The number of these is precisely fixed: a hundred are drawn from each district, and 'The Hundred' is the name they bear among their fellow-countrymen. Thus what was originally a mere number has come to be a title of distinction. The battle-line is made up of wedge-shaped formations. To give ground, provided that you return to the attack, is considered good tactics rather than cowardice. They bring back the bodies of the fallen even when a battle hangs in the balance. To throw away one's shield is the supreme disgrace, and the man who has thus dishonoured himself is debarred from attendance at sacrifice or assembly. Many such survivors from the battlefield have ended their shame by hanging themselves.

7

They choose their kings for their noble birth, their commanders for their valour. The power even of the kings is not absolute or arbitrary. The commanders rely on example rather than on the authority of their rank – on the admiration they win by showing conspicuous energy and courage and by pressing forward in front of their own troops. Capital punishment, imprisonment, even flogging, are allowed to none but the priests, and are not inflicted merely as punishments or on the commanders' orders, but as it were in obedience to the god whom the Germans believe to be present on the field of battle. They actually carry with them into the fight certain figures and emblems taken from their sacred groves. A specially powerful incitement to valour is that the squadrons and divisions are not made up at random by the mustering of chance-comers, but are each composed of men of one family or clan. Close by them, too, are their nearest and dearest, so that they can hear the shrieks of their women-folk and the wailing of their children. These are the witnesses whom each man reverences most highly, whose praise he most desires. It is to their mothers and wives that they go to have their wounds treated, and the women are not afraid to count and compare the gashes. They also carry supplies of food to the combatants and encourage them.

8

It stands on record that armies already wavering and on the point of collapse have been rallied by the women, pleading heroically with their men, thrusting forward their bared bosoms, and making them realize the imminent prospect of enslavement – a fate which the Germans fear more desperately for their women than for themselves. Indeed, you can secure a surer hold on these nations if you compel them to include among a consignment of hostages some girls of noble family. More than this, they believe that there resides in women an element of holiness and a gift of prophecy; and so they do not scorn to ask their advice, or lightly disregard their replies. In the reign of the emperor Vespasian we saw Veleda long honoured by many Germans as a divinity; and even earlier they showed a similar reverence for Aurinia and a number of others – a reverence untainted by servile flattery or any pretence of turning women into goddesses.

9

Above all other gods they worship Mercury, and count it no sin, on certain feast-days, to include human victims in the sacrifices offered to him. Hercules and Mars they appease by offerings of animals, in accordance with ordinary civilized custom. Some of the Suebi sacrifice also to Isis. I do not know the origin or explanation of this foreign cult; but the goddess's emblem, being made in the form of a light warship, itself proves that her worship came in from abroad. The Germans do not think it in keeping with the divine majesty to confine gods within walls or to portray them in the likeness of any human countenance. Their holy places are woods and groves, and they apply the names of deities to that hidden presence which is seen only by the eye of reverence.

10

For omens and the casting of lots they have the highest regard. Their procedure in casting lots is always the same. They cut off a branch of a nut-bearing tree and slice it into strips; these they mark with different signs and throw them completely at random onto a white cloth. Then the priest of the state, if the consultation is a public one, or the father of the family if it is private, offers a prayer to the gods, and looking up at the sky picks up three strips, one at a time, and reads their meaning from the signs previously scored on them. If the lots forbid an enterprise, there is no deliberation that day on the matter in question; if they allow it, confirmation by the taking of auspices is required. Although the familiar method of seeking information from the cries and the flight of birds is known to the Germans, they have also a special method of their own – to try to obtain omens and warnings from horses. These horses are kept at the public expense in the sacred woods and groves that I have mentioned; they are pure white and undefiled by any toil in the service of man. The priest and the king, or the chief of the state, yoke them to a sacred chariot and walk beside them, taking note of their neighs and snorts. No kind of omen inspires greater trust, not only among the common people, but even among the nobles and priests, who think that they themselves are but servants of the gods, whereas the horses are privy to the gods' counsels. There is yet another kind of omen-taking used to forecast the issue of serious wars. They contrive somehow to secure a captive from the nation with which they are at war and match him against a champion of their own, each being armed with his national weapons. The victory of one or the other is thought to forecast the issue of the war.

II

On matters of minor importance only the chiefs debate; on major affairs, the whole community. But even where the commons have the decision, the subject is considered in advance by the chiefs. Except in case of accident or emergency, they assemble on certain particular days, either shortly after the new moon or shortly before the full moon. These, they hold, are the most auspicious times for embarking on any enterprise. They do not reckon time by days, as we do, but by nights. All their engagements and appointments are made on this system. Night is regarded as ushering in the day. It is a drawback of their independent spirit that they do not take a summons as a command: instead of coming to a meeting all together, they waste two or three days by their unpunctuality. When the assembled crowd thinks fit, they take their seats fully armed. Silence is then commanded by the priests, who on such occasions have power to enforce obedience. Then such hearing is given to the king or state-chief as his age, rank, military distinction, or eloquence can secure – more because his advice carries weight than because he has the power to command. If a proposal displeases them, the people shout their dissent; if they approve, they clash their spears. To express approbation with their weapons is their most complimentary way of showing agreement.

12

The Assembly is competent also to hear criminal charges, especially those involving the risk of capital punishment. The mode of execution varies according to the offence. Traitors and deserters are hanged on trees; cowards, shirkers, and sodomites are pressed down under a wicker hurdle into the slimy mud of a bog. This distinction in the punishments is based on the idea that offenders against the state should be made a public example of, whereas deeds of shame should be buried out of men's sight. Less serious offences, too, have penalties proportioned to them. The man who is found guilty has to pay a fine of so many horses or cattle, part of which goes to the king or the state, part to the victim of the wrongful act or to his relatives. These same assemblies elect, among other officials, the magistrates who administer justice in the districts and villages. Each magistrate is assisted by a hundred assessors chosen from the people to advise him and to add weight to his decisions.

13

They transact no business, public or private, without being armed. But it is a rule that no one shall carry arms until the state authorities are satisfied that he will be competent to use them. Then, in the presence of the Assembly, either one of the chiefs or the young man's father or some other relative presents him with a shield and a spear. These, among the Germans, are the equivalent of the man's toga with us – the first distinction publicly conferred upon a youth, who now ceases to rank merely as a member of a household and becomes a citizen. Particularly noble birth, or great services rendered by their fathers, can obtain the rank of 'chief' for boys still in their teens. They are attached to others of more mature strength who have been approved some years before, and none of them blushes to be seen in a chief's retinue of followers. There are grades of rank even in these retinues, determined at the discretion of the chief whom they follow; and there is great rivalry, both among the followers to obtain the highest place in their leader's estimation and among the chiefs for the honour of having the biggest and most valiant retinue. Both prestige and power depend on being continually attended by a large train of picked young warriors, which is a distinction in peace and a protection in war. And it is not only in a chief's own nation that the superior number and quality of his retainers brings him glory and renown. Neighbouring states honour them also, courting them with embassies and complimenting them with presents. Very often the mere reputation of such men will virtually decide the issue of a war.

14

On the field of battle it is a disgrace to a chief to be surpassed in courage by his followers, and to the followers not to equal the courage of their chief. And to leave a battle alive after their chief has fallen means lifelong infamy and shame. To defend and protect him, and to let him get the credit for their own acts of heroism, are the most solemn obligations of their allegiance. The chiefs fight for victory, the followers for their chief. Many noble youths, if the land of their birth is stagnating in a long period of peace and inactivity, deliberately seek out other tribes which have some war in hand. For the Germans have no taste for peace; renown is more easily won among perils, and a large body of retainers cannot be kept together except by means of violence and war. They are always making demands on the generosity of their chief, asking for a coveted war-horse or a spear stained with the blood of a defeated enemy. Their meals, for which plentiful if homely fare is provided, count in lieu of pay. The wherewithal for this openhandedness comes from war and plunder. A German is not so easily prevailed upon to plough the land and wait patiently for harvest as to challenge a foe and earn wounds for his reward. He thinks it tame and spiritless to accumulate slowly by the sweat of his brow what can be got quickly by the loss of a little blood.

15

When not engaged in warfare they spend a certain amount of time in hunting, but much more in idleness, thinking of nothing else but sleeping and eating. For the boldest and most warlike men have no regular employment, the care of house, home, and fields being left to the women, old men, and weaklings of the family. In thus dawdling away their time they show a strange inconsistency – at one and the same time loving indolence and hating peace.

It is a national custom for gifts of cattle or agricultural produce to be made to the chiefs, individual citizens making voluntary contributions for this purpose. These are accepted as tokens of honour, but serve also to supply their wants. They take particular pleasure in gifts received from neighbouring states, such as are sent not only by individuals but by communities as well – choice horses, splendid arms, metal discs, and collars. And we have now taught them to accept presents of money also.

16

It is a well-known fact that the peoples of Germany never live in cities and will not even have their houses adjoin one another. They dwell apart, dotted about here and there, wherever a spring, plain, or grove takes their fancy.

Their villages are not laid out in the Roman style, with buildings adjacent and connected. Every man leaves an open space round his house, perhaps as a precaution against the risk of fire, perhaps because they are inexpert builders. They do not even make use of stones or wall-tiles; for all purposes they employ rough-hewn timber, ugly and unattractive-looking. Some parts, however, they carefully smear over with a clay of such purity and brilliance that it looks like painting or coloured design. They also have the habit of hollowing out underground caves, which they cover with masses of manure and use both as refuges from the winter and as storehouses for produce. Such shelters temper the keenness of the frosts; and if an invader comes, he ravages the open country, while these hidden excavations are either not known to exist, or else escape detection simply because they cannot be found without a search.

17

The universal dress in Germany is a cloak fastened with a brooch or, failing that, a thorn. They pass whole days by the fireside wearing no garment but this. It is a mark of great wealth to wear undergarments, which are not loose like those of the Sarmatians and Parthians, but fit tightly and follow the contour of every limb. They also wear the skins of wild animals – the tribes near the river frontiers without any regard to appearance, the more distant tribes with some refinement of taste, since in their part of the country there is no finery to be bought. These latter people select animals with care, and after stripping off the hides decorate them with patches of the skin of creatures that live in the unknown seas of the outer ocean. The dress of the women differs from that of the men in two respects only: women often wear outer garments of linen ornamented with a purple pattern; and as the upper part of these is sleeveless, the whole of their arms, and indeed the parts of their breasts nearest the shoulders, are exposed.

18

Their marriage code, however, is strict, and no feature of their morality deserves higher praise. They are almost unique among barbarians in being content with one wife apiece – all of them, that is, except a very few who take more than one wife not to satisfy their desires but because their exalted rank brings them many pressing offers of matrimonial alliances. The dowry is brought by husband to wife, not by wife to husband. Parents and kinsmen attend and approve the gifts – not gifts chosen to please a woman's fancy or gaily deck a young bride, but oxen, a horse with its bridle, or a shield, spear, and sword. In consideration of such gifts a man gets his wife, and she in her turn brings a present of arms to her husband. This interchange of gifts typifies for them the most sacred bond of union, sanctified by mystic rites under the favour of the presiding deities of wedlock. The woman must not think that she is excluded from aspirations to manly virtues or exempt from the hazards of warfare. That is why she is reminded, in the very ceremonies which bless her marriage at its outset, that she enters her husband's home to be the partner of his toils and perils, that both in peace and in war she is to share his sufferings and adventures. That is the meaning of the team of oxen, the horse ready for its rider, and the gift of arms. On these terms she must live her life and bear her children. She is receiving something that she must hand over intact and undepreciated to her children, something for her sons' wives to receive in their turn and pass on to her grandchildren.

19

By such means is the virtue of their women protected, and they live uncorrupted by the temptations of public shows or the excitements of banquets. Clandestine love-letters are unknown to men and women alike. Adultery is extremely rare, considering the size of the population. A guilty wife is summarily punished by her husband. He cuts off her hair, strips her naked, and in the presence of kinsmen turns her out of his house and flogs her all through the village. They have in fact no mercy on a wife who prostitutes her chastity. Neither beauty, youth, nor wealth can find her another husband. No one in Germany finds vice amusing, or calls it 'up-to-date' to seduce and be seduced. Even better is the practice of those states in which only virgins may marry, so that a woman who has once been a bride has finished with all such hopes and aspirations. She takes one husband, just as she has one body and one life. Her thoughts must not stray beyond him or her desires survive him. And even that husband she must love not for himself, but as an embodiment of the married state. To restrict the number of children, or to kill any of those born after the heir, is considered wicked. Good morality is more effective in Germany than good laws are elsewhere.

20

In every home the children go naked and dirty, and develop that strength of limb and tall stature which excite our admiration. Every mother feeds her child at the breast and does not depute the task to maids or nurses. The young master is not distinguished from the slave by any pampering in his upbringing. They live together among the same flocks and on the same earthen floor, until maturity sets apart the free and the spirit of valour claims them as her own. The young men are slow to mate, and thus they reach manhood with vigour unimpaired. The girls, too, are not hurried into marriage. As old and full-grown as the men, they match their mates in age and strength, and the children inherit the robustness of their parents. The sons of sisters are as highly honoured by their uncles as by their own fathers. Some tribes even consider the former tie the closer and more sacred of the two, and in demanding hostages prefer nephews to sons, thinking that this gives them a firmer grip on men's hearts and a wider hold on the family. However, a man's heirs and successors are his own children, and there is no such thing as a will. When there is no issue, the first in order of succession are brothers, and then uncles, first on the father's, then on the mother's side. The more relatives and connections by marriage a man has, the greater authority he commands in old age. There is nothing to be gained by childlessness in Germany.

21

Heirs are under an obligation to take up both the feuds and the friendships of a father or kinsman. But feuds do not continue for ever unreconciled. Even homicide can be atoned for by a fixed number of cattle or sheep, the compensation being received by the whole family. This is to the advantage of the community: for private feuds are particularly dangerous where there is such complete liberty.

No nation indulges more freely in feasting and entertaining than the German. It is accounted a sin to turn any man away from your door. The host welcomes his guest with the best meal that his means allow. When he has finished entertaining him, the host undertakes a fresh role: he accompanies the guest to the nearest house where further hospitality can be had. It makes no difference that they come uninvited; they are welcomed just as warmly. No distinction is ever made between acquaintance and stranger as far as the right to hospitality is concerned. As the guest takes his leave, it is customary to let him have anything he asks for; and the host, with as little hesitation, will ask for a gift in return. They take delight in presents, but they expect no repayment for giving them and feel no obligation in receiving them.

22

As soon as they wake, which is often well after sunrise, they wash, generally with warm water – as one might expect in a country where winter lasts so long. After washing they eat a meal, each man having a separate seat and table. Then they go out to attend to any business they have in hand, or, as often as not, to partake in a feast – always with their weapons about them. Drinking-bouts lasting all day and all night are not considered in any way disgraceful. The quarrels that inevitably arise over the cups are seldom settled merely by hard words, but more often by killing and wounding. Nevertheless, they often make a feast an occasion for discussing such affairs as the ending of feuds, the arrangement of marriage alliances, the adoption of chiefs, and even questions of peace or war. At no other time, they think, is the heart so open to sincere feelings or so quick to warm to noble sentiments. The Germans are not cunning or sophisticated enough to refrain from blurting out their inmost thoughts in the freedom of festive surroundings, so that every man's soul is laid completely bare. On the following day the subject is reconsidered, and thus due account is taken of both occasions. They debate when they are incapable of pretence but reserve their decision for a time when they cannot well make a mistake.

23

Their drink is a liquor made from barley or other grain, which is fermented to produce a certain resemblance to wine. Those who dwell nearest the Rhine or the Danube also buy wine. Their food is plain – wild fruit, fresh game, and curdled milk. They satisfy their hunger without any elaborate cuisine or appetizers. But they do not show the same self-control in slaking their thirst. If you indulge their intemperance by plying them with as much drink as they desire, they will be as easily conquered by this besetting weakness as by force of arms.

24

They have only one kind of public show, which is performed without variation at every festive gathering. Naked youths, trained to the sport, dance about among swords and spears levelled at them. Practice begets skill, and skill grace; but they are not professionals and do not receive payment. Their most daring flings have their only reward in the pleasure they give the spectators. They play at dice – surprisingly enough – when they are sober, making a serious business of it; and they are so reckless in their anxiety to win, however often they lose, that when everything else is gone they will stake their personal liberty on a last decisive throw. A loser willingly discharges his debt by becoming a slave: even though he

may be the younger and stronger man, he allows himself
to be bound and sold by the winner. Such is their stub-
born persistence in a vicious practice – though they call it
'honour'. Slaves of this description are disposed of by
way of trade, since even their owners want to escape the
shame of such a victory.

25

Slaves in general do not have particular duties about the
house and estate allotted to them, as our slaves do. Each
has control of a holding and home of his own. The master
demands from him a stated quantity of grain, live-stock,
or cloth, as he would from a tenant. To this extent the
slave is under an obligation of service; but all other
duties, including household work, are carried out by the
housewife and her children. To flog a slave, or to punish
him by imprisonment and hard labour, is very unusual;
yet to kill one outright is quite common. But they do this,
not as a strict enforcement of discipline, but in a fit of
passion, as they might kill an enemy – except that they do
not have to pay for it. Freedmen rank little higher than
slaves: they seldom have any influence in a household,
never in the state, except among the tribes that are ruled
by kings. There they rise above free men and even above
noblemen. Elsewhere, the inferior status of freedmen is a
proof of genuine liberty.

26

The employment of capital in order to increase it by

usury is unknown in Germany; and ignorance is here a surer defence than any prohibition. Lands proportioned to their own number are appropriated in turn for tillage by the whole body of tillers. They then divide them among themselves according to rank; the division is made easy by the wide tracts of cultivable ground available. These ploughlands are changed yearly, and still there is enough and to spare. The fact is that although their land is fertile and extensive, they fail to take full advantage of it because they do not work sufficiently hard. They do not plant orchards, fence off meadows, or irrigate gardens; the only demand they make upon the soil is to produce a corn-crop. Hence even the year itself is not divided by them into as many seasons as it is with us: winter, spring, and summer are the seasons they understand and have names for; the name of autumn is as completely unknown to them as are the blessings that it can bring.

27

There is no ostentation about their funerals. The only special observance is that the bodies of famous men are burned with particular kinds of wood. When they have heaped up the pyre they do not throw garments or spices on it; only the dead man's arms, and sometimes his horse too, are cast into the flames. The tomb is a raised mound of turf. They disdain to show honour by laboriously rearing high monuments of stone, which they think would only lie heavy on the dead. Weeping and wailing are soon abandoned, sorrow and mourning not so soon. A woman may decently express her grief; a man should nurse his in his heart.

Such is the general account that we find given of the origin and customs of the Germans as a whole. I shall now point out how far the individual tribes differ from one another in their institutions and practices, and which of them have migrated from Germany into Gaul.

28

That the power of Gaul once exceeded that of Germany is recorded by that greatest of authorities, Julius Caesar; and therefore we may well believe that there were also migrations of Gauls into Germany. There was only a river between – a trifling obstacle to prevent any tribe that grew strong enough from seizing fresh lands, and afterwards perhaps exchanging them for others, when they were no one's property and not yet partitioned between powerful monarchies. Thus, between the Hercynian forest and the rivers Rhine and Main, we find the Helvetii in occupation, and beyond them the Boii, both Celtic peoples. This land is still called Bohemia, which attests the ancient tradition concerning it, although the inhabitants have since changed. Whether the Aravisci came as immigrants to Pannonia from the tribe of the Osi, or the Osi from the Aravisci into Germany – both peoples still speak the same language and have the same customs and character – cannot be determined, since there was in those days the same poverty and the same freedom on both banks of the Danube, so that the attractions and disadvantages were identical. The Treviri and Nervii even take pride in the German descent to which they lay claim. Such a glorious origin, they feel, should prevent their being thought to resemble the unwarlike Gauls. The actual bank of the Rhine is held by peoples of undoubted German origin – the Vangiones, the Triboci, and the Nemetes. Even the Ubii, for all that they have earned the rank of a Roman colony and like to call themselves Agrippinenses after their foundress Agrippina, are not ashamed of their ancestry. They crossed the river many years ago, and as they had given proof of their loyalty to Rome they were stationed close to the west bank, to keep out intruders, not to be kept under surveillance themselves.

29

The most conspicuously brave of all the German tribes in Gaul, the Batavi, hold little of the river-bank, but do hold the Rhine island. They were once a section of the Chatti, and on the occasion of a civil war they migrated to their present home – destined there to become a part of the Roman empire. But they still retain an honourable privilege in token of their ancient alliance with us. They are not subjected to the indignity of tribute or ground down by the tax-gatherer. Free from imposts and special levies, and reserved for employment in battle, they are like weapons and armour – 'only to be used in war'. We

exercise the same suzerainty over the Mattiaci; for the
greatness of Rome has spread the awe of her empire even
beyond the Rhine and the old frontiers. In geographical
position they are on the German side, in heart and soul
they are with us. They resemble the Batavi in every way,
except that their country and climate give an even keener
edge to their spirit.

I am not inclined to reckon among the peoples of
Germany the cultivators of the *agri decumates*, although
they have established themselves between the Rhine and
the Danube. All the most disreputable characters in
Gaul, all the penniless adventurers, seized on a territory
that was a kind of no man's land. It was only later,
when the frontier line of defence was drawn and the
garrisons moved forward, that they came to be regarded
as an outlying corner of the empire and a part of a
province.

30

Beyond them dwell the Chatti, whose country starts from
the Hercynian forest; it is less open and less marshy than
the other states that stretch across the wide plains of
Germany. For the hills run on and only thin out
gradually; and the Hercynian forest, like a nurse with her
infant cares, escorts its Chatti throughout and finally
sets them down at the edge of the plains. This nation is
distinguished by hardy bodies, well-knit limbs, fierce
countenances, and unusual mental vigour. They have
plenty of judgement and discernment, measured by

German standards. They appoint picked men to lead them, and then obey them. They know how to keep rank, and how to recognize an opportunity – or else postpone their attack. They can map out the duties of the day and make sure the defences of the night. They know that fortune is not to be relied on, but only valour; and – the rarest thing of all, which the gods have vouchsafed only to a military discipline like the Roman – they place more confidence in their general than in their troops.

All their strength lies in their infantry, which, in addition to its arms, is burdened with entrenching-tools and provisions. Other tribes may be seen going forth to battle; the Chatti come out for a campaign. They seldom engage in swift rushes or in casual fighting – tactics which properly belong to cavalry, with its quick successes and quick retreats. Speed suggests something very like fear, whereas deliberate movement rather indicates a steady courage.

31

There is one custom – sometimes practised by other German tribes, though rarely, and only as an exhibition of individual daring – that has become a general rule among the Chatti. As soon as they reach manhood they let their hair and beard grow as they will. This fashion of covering the face is assumed in accordance with a vow pledging them to the service of Valour; and only when they have slain an enemy do they lay it aside. Standing over the bloody corpse they have despoiled, they reveal their faces to the world once more, and proclaim that they have at last repaid the debt they owe for being brought into the world and have proved themselves worthy of their native land and parents. The coward who will not fight must stay unshorn. The bravest also wear an iron ring – which in their country is a great indignity – as a mark of servitude, until they release themselves by killing a man. But many of the Chatti like these fashions, and even greybeards can be seen thus distinguished, for foe and fellow-countryman alike to point at. Every battle is begun by these men. They are always in the front rank, where they present a startling sight: for even in peace-time they will not soften the ferocity of their expression. None of them has a home, land, or any occupation. To whatever host they choose to go, they get their keep from him, squandering other men's property since they think it beneath them to have any of their own, until old age leaves them without enough blood in their veins for such stern heroism.

32

Close to the Chatti are the Usipi and the Tencteri. They dwell on the bank of the Rhine, which by this time flows in a well-defined channel and is large enough to serve as a boundary. The Tencteri, besides sharing in the general military distinction, excel in skilful horsemanship. The infantry of the Chatti are not more famous than the cavalry of the Tencteri. This tradition was started by their ancestors, whom they still continue to emulate. The children play at riding; the grown men compete in riding; even the old will not give it up. Horses pass by inheritance along with slaves, homestead, and rights of succession. The horses go to a son, not necessarily, like the rest of the property, to the eldest, but to the one who is the keenest and ablest soldier.

33

Next to the Tencteri came the Bructeri in former times; but now the Chamavi and Angrivarii are said to have moved into their territory. The Bructeri were defeated and almost annihilated by a coalition of neighbouring tribes. Perhaps they were hated for their domineering pride; or it may have been the lure of booty, or some special favour accorded us by the gods. We were even permitted to witness the battle. More than 60,000 were killed, not by Roman swords or javelins, but – more splendid still – as a spectacle before our delighted eyes. Long, I pray, may foreign nations persist, if not in loving us, at least in hating one another; for destiny is driving our empire upon its appointed path, and fortune can bestow on us no better gift than discord among our foes.

34

The Angrivarii and Chamavi have a common frontier on one side with the Dulgubnii, Chasuarii, and other tribes of no special fame, while on the north-west they are succeeded by the Frisii, who comprise a larger section and a smaller section, called respectively the Greater and the Lesser Frisii. Both sections have the Rhine as a frontier right down to the Ocean, and their settlements also extend round vast lagoons, which have been sailed by Roman fleets. We have even ventured upon the Northern Ocean itself, and rumour has it that there are Pillars of Hercules in the far north. It may be that Hercules did go there; or perhaps it is only that we by common consent ascribe any remarkable achievement in any place to his famous name. Drusus Germanicus did not lack the courage of the explorer, but Ocean forbade further research into its own secrets or those of Hercules. Since then no one has attempted it. It has been judged more pious and reverent to believe in the alleged exploits of gods than to establish the true facts.

35

This is as far as the Germany we know extends to the west. To the north it falls away in a huge bend; and here at once we come to the nation of the Chauci. They begin after the Frisii and hold a section of the coast; but they also lie along the flanks of all those nations that I have been describing, and finally curve back to meet the Chatti. This huge stretch of country is not merely occupied, but filled to overflowing, by the Chauci. They are the noblest people of Germany, and one that prefers to maintain its greatness by righteous dealing. Untouched by greed or lawless ambition, they dwell in quiet seclusion, never provoking a war, never robbing or plundering their neighbours. It is conspicuous proof of their valour and

strength that their superiority does not rest on aggression.
Yet every man of them has arms ready to his hand, and
if occasion demands it they have vast reserves of men and
horses. So their reputation stands as high in peace as in
war.

36

On the flank of the Chauci and the Chatti, the Cherusci
have been left free from attack to enjoy a prolonged
peace, too secure and enervating – a pleasant but perilous
indulgence among powerful aggressors, where there can
be no true peace. When force decides everything, for-
bearance and righteousness are qualities attributed only to
the strong; and so the Cherusci, once known as 'good,
honest people', now hear themselves called lazy fools,
while the luck of the victorious Chatti passes for profound
wisdom. The fall of the Cherusci involved also the
neighbouring tribe of the Fosi, who played second fiddle
to them in prosperity but get an equal share of their
adversity.

37

In the same corner of Germany, nearest to the open sea,
dwell the Cimbri, a name mighty in history, though now
they are only a little state. Widespread traces of their
ancient fame may still be seen: huge encampments on
both sides of the Rhine, by their enormous circuit, still
give a measure of the mass and man-power of the nation
and demonstrate the historical truth of that great exodus.

Rome was in her six hundred and fortieth year when the alarm of the Cimbrian arms was first heard, in the consulship of Caecilius Metellus and Papirius Carbo. Reckoning from that year to the second consulship of the emperor Trajan, we get a total of about two hundred and ten years. Such is the time it is taking to conquer Germany. In this long period much punishment has been given and taken. Neither by the Samnites nor by the Carthaginians, not by Spain or Gaul, or even by the Parthians, have we had more lessons taught us. The freedom of Germany is capable of more energetic action than the Arsacid despotism. After all, what has the East to taunt us with, except the slaughter of Crassus? And it soon lost its own prince Pacorus and was humbled at the feet of Ventidius. But the Germans routed or captured Carbo, Cassius, Aurelius Scaurus, Servilius Caepio, and Mallius Maximus, and robbed the Republic, almost at one stroke, of five consular armies. Even from Augustus they took Varus and his three legions. And we had to pay a high price for the defeats inflicted upon them by Gaius Marius in Italy, by Julius Caesar in Gaul, and by Drusus, Tiberius, and Germanicus in their own country. The boastful threats of Gaius Caesar ended in farce. After that came a lull, until the Germans took advantage of our dissensions and civil wars to storm the quarters of the legions and make a bid for possession of Gaul. This attempt ended in another defeat for them; but the more recent 'victories' claimed by our commanders have been little more than excuses for celebrating triumphs.

38

We must now speak of the Suebi, who do not, like the Chatti or the Tencteri, constitute a single nation. They occupy more than half Germany, and are divided into a number of separate tribes under different names, though all are called by the generic title of 'Suebi'. It is a special characteristic of this nation to comb the hair sideways and tie it in a knot. This distinguishes the Suebi from the rest of the Germans, and, among the Suebi, distinguishes the freeman from the slave. Individual men of other tribes adopt the same fashion, either because they are related in some way to the Suebi, or merely because the imitative instinct is so strong in human beings; but even these few abandon it when they are no longer young. The Suebi keep it up till they are grey-headed; the hair is twisted back so that it stands erect, and is often knotted on the very crown of the head. The chiefs use an even more elaborate style. But this concern about their personal appearance is altogether innocent. These are no love-locks to entice women to accept their advances. Their elaborate coiffure is intended to give them greater height, so as to look more terrifying to their foes when they are about to go into battle.

39

The oldest and most famous of the Suebi, it is said, are the Semnones, and their antiquity is confirmed by a religious observance. At a set time, deputations from all the tribes of the same stock gather in a grove hallowed by the auguries of their ancestors and by immemorial awe. The sacrifice of a human victim in the name of all marks the grisly opening of their savage ritual. Another observance shows their reverence for this grove. No one may enter it unless he is bound with a cord, by which he acknowledges his own inferiority and the power of the deity. Should he chance to fall, he may not raise himself or get up again, but must roll out over the ground. The grove is the centre of their whole religion. It is regarded as the cradle of the race and the dwelling-place of the supreme god to whom all things are subject and obedient. The Semnones gain prestige from their prosperity. The districts they inhabit number a hundred, and their multitude makes them believe that they are the principal people of the Suebi.

40

The Langobardi, by contrast, are famous because they are so few. Hemmed in as they are by many mighty peoples, they find safety, not in submission, but in facing the risks of battle. After them come the Reudigni, Aviones, Anglii, Varini, Eudoses, Suarines, and Nuitones, all of them safe behind ramparts of rivers and woods. There is nothing noteworthy about these tribes individually, but they share a common worship of Nerthus, or Mother Earth. They believe that she takes part in human affairs, riding in a chariot among her people. On an island of the sea stands an inviolate grove, in which, veiled with a cloth, is a chariot that none but the priest may touch. The priest can feel the presence of the goddess in this holy of holies, and attends her with deepest reverence as her chariot is drawn along by cows. Then follow days of rejoicing and merrymaking in every place that she condescends to visit and sojourn in. No one goes to war, no one takes up arms; every iron object is locked away. Then, and then only, are peace and quiet known and welcomed, until the goddess, when she has had enough of the society of men, is restored to her sacred precinct by the priest. After that, the chariot, the vestments, and (believe it if you will) the goddess herself, are cleansed in a secluded lake. This service is performed by slaves who are immediately afterwards drowned in the lake. Thus mystery begets terror and a pious reluctance to ask what that sight can be which is seen only by men doomed to die.

41

The section of the Suebian territory that I have described stretches out into the less-known part of Germany. Nearer to us – to follow now the course of the Danube as we previously followed that of the Rhine – are our faithful allies the Hermunduri. Because they are so loyal, they are the only Germans who trade with us not merely on the river bank but far within our borders, and indeed in the splendid colony that is the capital of Raetia. They come over where they will, and without a guard set over them. The other Germans are only allowed to see our armed camps; to the Hermunduri we exhibit our mansions and country-houses without their coveting them. In their country are the sources of the Elbe, a river well known and much talked of in earlier days, but now a mere name.

42

Next to the Hermunduri dwell the Naristi, followed by the Marcomanni and the Quadi. The Marcomanni are conspicuous in reputation and power: even their home-land, from which they drove out the Boii, was won by their bravery. Nor do the Naristi and Quadi fall below their high standard. These peoples form the front, so to speak, presented to us by that part of Germany which is girdled by the Danube. Down to our own times the Marcomanni and Quadi still had kings of their own race, the noble line of Maroboduus and Tudrus; but now they sometimes have foreign rulers set over them. The power of the kings depends entirely on the authority of Rome. They occasionally receive armed assistance from us, more often financial aid, which proves equally effective.

43

Close behind the Marcomanni and Quadi are the Marsigni, Cotini, Osi, and Buri. Of these, the Marsigni and Buri are exactly like the Suebi in language and mode of life. The Cotini and the Osi are not Germans: that is proved by their languages, Celtic in the one case, Pannonian in the other, and also by the fact that they submit to paying tribute. The payments are exacted from them, as foreigners, by the Quadi and by the Sarmatians respectively – of which the Cotini have all the more reason to be ashamed inasmuch as they work iron mines. All these peoples are settled in country with few plains, consisting mostly of mountains and upland valleys. Suebia, in fact, is cut in two down the middle by an unbroken range of mountains, beyond which live a multitude of tribes, of whom the Lugii are the most widely spread, being divided into a number of smaller units. I need only give the names of the most powerful: the Harii, Helvecones, Manimi, Helisii, and Naharvali.

The Naharvali proudly point out a grove associated with an ancient worship. The presiding priest dresses like a woman; but the deities are said to be the counterpart of our Castor and Pollux. This indicates their character, but their name is the Alci. There are no images, and nothing to suggest that the cult is of foreign origin; but they are certainly worshipped as young men and as brothers.

As for the Harii, not only are they superior in strength to the other peoples I have just mentioned, but they minister to their savage instincts by trickery and clever timing. They black their shields and dye their bodies, and choose pitch dark nights for their battles. The shadowy, awe-inspiring appearance of such a ghoulish army inspires mortal panic; for no enemy can endure a sight so strange and hellish. Defeat in battle starts always with the eyes.

44

Beyond the Lugii are the Gothones, who are governed by kings. Their rule is somewhat more autocratic than in the other German states, but not to such a degree that freedom is destroyed. Then, immediately bordering on the sea, are the Rugii and Lemovii. All these peoples are distinguished by the use of round shields and short swords, and by submission to regal authority.

Next come the states of the Suiones, right out in the sea. They are powerful not only in arms and men but also in fleets. The shape of their ships differs from the normal in having a prow at each end, so that they are always facing the right way to put in to shore. They do not propel them with sails, nor do they fasten a row of oars to the sides. The rowlocks are movable, as one finds them on some river craft, and can be reversed, as circumstances require, for rowing in either direction. Wealth, too, is held in high honour; and so a single monarch rules, with no restrictions on his power and with an unquestioned claim to obedience. Arms are not, as in the rest of Germany, allowed to all and sundry, but are kept in charge of a custodian – who in fact is a slave. There are two reasons for this control of weapons: the sea makes sudden invasion impossible, and idle crowds of armed men easily get into mischief. As for not putting any noble or freeman, or even a freedman, in charge of the arms – that is a part of royal policy.

45

Beyond the Suiones we find another sea, sluggish and almost stagnant. This sea is believed to be the boundary that girdles the earth because the last radiance of the setting sun lingers on here till dawn, with a brilliance that dims the stars. Popular belief adds that you can hear the sound he makes as he rises from the waves and can see the shape of his horses and the rays on his head. So far and no farther (in this, report speaks truly) does the world extend. Turning, therefore, to the right hand shore of the Suebian sea, we find it washing the country of the Aestii, who have the same customs and fashions as the Suebi, but a language more like the British. They worship the Mother of the gods, and wear, as an emblem of this cult, the device of a wild boar, which stands them in stead of armour or human protection and gives the worshipper a sense of security even among his enemies. They seldom use weapons of iron, but clubs very often. They cultivate grain and other crops with a perseverance unusual among the indolent Germans. They also ransack the sea. They are the only people who collect amber – *glaesum* is their own word for it – in the shallows or even on the beach. Like true barbarians, they have never asked or discovered what it is or how it is produced. For a long time, indeed, it lay unheeded like any other refuse of the sea, until Roman luxury made its reputation. They have no use for it themselves. They gather it crude, pass it on in unworked lumps, and are astounded at the price it fetches. Amber, however, is certainly a gum of trees, as you may see from the fact that creeping and even winged creatures are often seen shining through it. Caught in the sticky liquid, they were then imprisoned as it hardened. I imagine that in the islands and continents of the west, just as in the secret chambers of the east, where the trees exude frankincense and balm, there must be woods and groves of unusual productivity. Their gums, drawn out by the rays of their near neighbour the sun, flow in liquid state into the adjacent sea and are finally washed up by violent storms on the shores that lie opposite. If you test the properties of amber by applying fire to it, you will find that it lights like a torch and burns with a smoky, pungent flame, soon becoming a semi-fluid mass like pitch or resin.

Bordering on the Suiones are the nations of the Sitones. They resemble them in all respects but one – woman is the ruling sex. That is the measure of their decline, I will not say below freedom, but even below decent slavery.

46

Here Suebia ends. I do not know whether to class the tribes of the Peucini, Venedi, and Fenni with the Germans or with the Sarmatians. The Peucini, however, who are sometimes called Bastarnae, are like Germans in their language, manner of life, and mode of settlement and habitation. Squalor is universal among them and their nobles are indolent. Mixed marriages are giving them something of the repulsive appearance of the Sarmatians. The Venedi have adopted many Sarmatian habits; for their plundering forays take them over all the wooded and mountainous highlands that lie between the Peucini and the Fenni. Nevertheless, they are on the whole to be classed as Germans; for they have settled homes, carry shields, and are fond of travelling – and travelling fast – on foot, differing in all these respects from the Sarmatians, who live in wagons or on horseback. The Fenni are astonishingly savage and disgustingly poor. They have no proper weapons, no horses, no homes. They eat wild herbs, dress in skins, and sleep on the ground. Their only hope of getting better fare lies in their arrows, which, for lack of iron, they tip with bone. The women support themselves by hunting, exactly like the men; they accompany them everywhere and insist on taking their share in bringing down the game. The only way they have of protecting their infants against wild beasts or bad weather is to hide them under a makeshift covering of interlaced branches. Such is the shelter to which the young folk come back and in which the old must lie. Yet they count their lot happier than that of others who groan over field labour, sweat over house-building, or hazard their own and other men's fortunes in the hope of profit and the fear of loss. Unafraid of anything that man or god can do to them, they have reached a state that few human beings can attain: for these men are so well content that they do not even need to pray for anything. What comes after them is the stuff of fables – Hellusii and Oxiones with the faces and features of men, the bodies and limbs of animals. On such unverifiable stories I shall express no opinion.

NOTES ON THE AGRICOLA

The extant manuscripts of the *Agricola* are few in number:

    (1) and (2) Vatican, late 15th century.

    (3) Toledo Chapter Library, late 15th century.

    (4) Library of Count Balleani at Jesi, near Ancona. This mid 9th century manuscript, rediscovered in 1902, is the ultimate source of (1), (2), and (3). The 9th century text is incomplete, the beginning and the end having been added by a 15th century hand; and it was evidently copied from an original that contained many errors. But it remains our most valuable source.

The text followed in this translation is in the main that of Ogilvie and Richmond (Oxford Press, 1967). Notes refer to some passages where the OR text has been departed from, or where some special textual difficulty calls for comment.

Chapter 4, 'he was tempted to drink deeper': The Romans from of old distrusted philosophy as an enemy of the active life. More than once in the Republican period philosophers were ordered to leave Rome. Under the Empire, philosophy was sometimes a cover for opposition to Government, and was resented as such. Domitian expelled philosophers on at least one occasion.

Chapter 5, 'his staff-captaincy': The phrase *titulus tribunatus* seems to mean that Agricola, while holding the rank of *tribunus militum*, was not assigned to any particular legion. An unassigned tribune could obviously be more easily spared.

Chapter 6, 'the ballot': When elected to a quaestorship a man drew his particular post by lot. It might be either in Rome or in the provinces.

    'strengthened his position': Because special privileges were allotted to fathers of children. Agricola probably was enabled to hold a praetorship one year before the usual age of thirty.

'no judicial duties': The *iurisdictio* which had been the main function of praetors under the Republic still belonged to a few of them, notably to the *praetor urbanus* and *praetor peregrinus*. The task of organizing public games was exclusively assigned to the praetors by Augustus.

'he repaired the losses': After the great fire at Rome in A.D. 64, Nero had pillaged temples throughout the empire. Private individuals and even public officials (Vitellius, for example, when he was commissioner of temples and public buildings) followed his bad example. Agricola, acting as a special commissioner, recovered all that could be recovered. The major depredations of Nero were past hope of recovery.

Chapter 9, 'sullenness or arrogance': Many editors delete *tristitiam et adrogantiam et avaritiam exuerat* as a marginal note meant to explain *nulla ultra potestatis persona*; but a fair sense can be got by emphasizing the force of the pluperfect tense *exuerat*. However, in view of the sentence lower down – 'To mention incorruptibility' etc. – the words *et avaritiam* are probably an interpolation.

'his colleagues': If the word is used strictly, it can refer only to the governors of neighbouring provinces; and that may be the meaning. But as attention is concentrated on the internal affairs of Aquitania, it may be used loosely to include the other *legati* who, strictly speaking, were subordinates of Agricola. The procurators were the financial agents of the emperor.

Chapter 10, 'The general shape of Britain': If you bisect a diamond-shaped figure along its longer axis and produce that axis to form a 'handle', you have one type of double-headed axe. If Tacitus is correctly reporting Livy and Fabius Rusticus, we must admit that their comparisons are not apt, since hardly anyone has been able to see how Britain south of the Forth and Clyde resembles either of these objects. But OR's attempt to emend and reinterpret the text so as to make it describe triangular objects is unconvincing.

Chapter 11, 'Gauls settled in the island': The Celtic immigrants into Britain came in at least three waves:

> (a) Goidelic Celts – perhaps as early as 900 B.C.
> (b) Brittonic Celts – from about 600 B.C.
> (c) Belgae from Gaul – from the end of the second century B.C.

From dialects of Goidelic Celts come Gaelic, Irish, and Manx; from Brittonic dialects, Welsh, Cornish, and Breton.

'History tells us': The Gauls, when attacked by Julius Caesar, were still a vigorous and warlike people. But the tide had already turned: they were no longer moving east across the Rhine, and German tribes were pressing westwards against them. The Gauls soon settled down to Roman rule. It is curious that Tacitus should scoff at them for doing so.

Chapter 12, 'kings': Quite a number of British kings are known from native coins – e.g. Cunobelinus (Cymbeline), Commius, Tincommius, Tasciovanus, Verica.

'passes along the horizon': Tacitus, who seems to have been uninterested in and somewhat ignorant of certain scientific facts widely known in the ancient world, is imagining a disc-like earth, although its spherical shape was known to Greek scientists as early as the fourth century B.C., and through them to many Romans. He apparently thought that the sun passed across just below the horizon, and that the flat edges of the earth were not high enough to cast shadows to the sky; hence the night glow in the extreme north.

'The soil will produce': Reading *patiens frugum fecundumque.*

'pearls': Julius Caesar is said to have dedicated a breastplate decorated with British pearls in the temple of Venus Genetrix at Rome.

Chapter 14, 'a colony of veterans': Camulodunum (Colchester), founded under Ostorius Scapula in A.D. 50.

'Cogidumnus': A famous inscription from Chichester mentions 'Ti. Claudius Cogidubnus, king, legate of Augustus in Britain'.

Chapter 15, 'the Germans': Referring to the Cherusci, who under Arminius in A.D. 9 destroyed three Roman legions commanded by P. Quinctilius Varus. The river is of course the Rhine.

'their deified Julius': *Divus* was regularly prefixed to the name of a deceased emperor who had been deified. Ordinarily this is merely a formality; but in this passage there may well be a sarcastic point in *Divus*.

'success': The word *felicibus* is omitted in the Vatican manuscripts, producing a completely different and much less appropriate sense. A good illustration of the superiority of the Jesi manuscript.

Chapter 19, 'tricks of profiteers': The proceedings of the Roman profiteers, who might include any official from a governor downwards, are somewhat obscure, though certainly nefarious. The requisition of corn was, it seems, made by the governor and was additional to the tribute paid in money. There were two main abuses:

> (a) Where corn was scarce, the natives had to go through a form of buying from the Romans the corn they were obligated to deliver. Actually it stayed in the public granaries all the time, and they had to lose the difference between the high prices they were forced to

pay for it and the low prices they received for it from the officials.

(b) Where corn was plentiful, the natives were told to deliver it, at great inconvenience and expense, to distant places. They presumably paid the officials to release them from this obligation.

Chapter 20, 'garrisoned forts': Mainly for the protection of the newly-surrendered Britons against their unconquered fellow-countrymen.

'with so little interference': Reading *nulla ... pars pariter inlacessita*. The manuscripts, followed by OR, omit *pariter*. But without some such word the sentence is very harsh.

Chapter 22, 'establishment of forts': For details of these forts, see OR p. 59, together with the map on p. 58 and the key to the sites on pp. 338–9.

Chapter 23, 'the valour of our army and the glory of Rome': Perhaps only a euphemism for Agricola's ambition.

'The Clyde and the Forth': A natural line of defence. North of it no natural frontier can be found: the whole island would need to be conquered and held.

Chapter 24, 'started ... by crossing the river Annan': The manuscripts have *nave prima transgressus*, from which it is difficult to extract a satisfactory sense, although OR try to do so. For *nave prima* suggests a water-borne operation of some magnitude; and this would have to be either (1) an expedition across the Solway Firth to the coast of Galloway (assuming that Agricola had withdrawn southwards for the winter, probably to York), or (2) an expedition down the Clyde to the coast of Ayrshire (assuming that he wintered somewhere on the Forth–Clyde line). In either case, it seems surprising that he should have incurred the trouble and danger of a movement by sea when he could have gone much more easily by land. The reading adopted in this translation is based on a conjecture of Richmond's, carried further by K. Wellesley in *Journal of Roman Studies*, 1969. The suggestion is that *nave prima* is a corruption of *Anavam primum*, or something similar. The Anava is the river Annan in Dumfriesshire; and the possibility that Agricola followed this particular route in opening his fifth campaign is strengthened by the discovery of a large Agricolan fort at Dalswinton, about eight miles west of the Annan.

'have now become better known': Reading *melius aditus portusque ... cogniti*. The manuscripts have *in melius*, which is bracketed as an interpolation by OR.

Chapter 25, 'threatening movements by the enemy on land': The original reading of the Jesi manuscript – *infesta hostilis exercitus itinera* – gives a satisfactory sense. OR adopt the marginal correction *hostili exercitu*.

Chapter 26, 'the men of the ninth': Another clear case of the superiority of the Jesi manuscript: instead of *nonanis* the Vatican manuscripts have *Romanis*.

Chapter 28, 'a memorable exploit': There is no clear indication of the point from which the Usipi started. Probably they set out from the west coast and sailed north and east round Cape Wrath to end up on the shores of Denmark or northern Germany.

'one of these escaped and went back': The manuscripts have *uno remigante*, which is retained 'with misgiving' by OR. But nearly all editors have regarded the sense 'with one rowing' as unsatisfactory. If, as Tacitus seems to imply, all three ships were eventually lost through bad seamanship, it looks as if the surviving pilot was not on board at the end of the voyage. In that case the old emendation *uno remigrante* may well be right. Many others have been proposed.

Chapter 29, 'Mount Graupius': The actual site of the battle cannot be established. But the discovery of a series of camp-sites, including some of a known Agricolan pattern, along the east coast as far north as Banffshire has convinced modern scholars that it was not far from the coast lying east of the Moray Firth. The name of the Grampian mountains reproduces a misspelling of *Graupium* in the first edition of the *Agricola*, printed near the end of the fifteenth century.

'old age was fresh and green': A quotation from Virgil's description of Charon in *Aeneid* VI, 304.

Chapter 31, 'to slave in other lands': Cohorts of Britons served in Germany, Pannonia, and elsewhere.

'Our wives and sisters': The most famous case is that of Boudicca, widow of Prasutagus, client king of the Iceni in East Anglia. After her husband's death in A.D. 61 she and her daughters are alleged to have been outraged by Roman underlings (Tacitus, *Annals* XIV, 31).

'The Brigantes': There is no other evidence that the Brigantes, whose client queen at this time was Cartimandua, took any part in the rising of Boudicca, which was mainly the work of the Iceni and the Trinovantes (in Essex) – though it is true that in Chapter 18 Tacitus calls it *rebellio totius Britanniae*. It has been suggested that he deliberately puts into the mouth of Calgacus what might seem a natural error, since the Brigantes were much nearer to him and also much more powerful than the other tribes. But more probably the mistake is Tacitus's own: he seems to have momentarily confused two famous British royal ladies. In A.D. 50 or 51 Cartimandua actually surrendered the patriot Caratacus to the Romans and accepted Roman aid against her own rebellious subjects.

'to avenge past injuries': The manuscripts have *non in paenitentiam laturi*, which is certainly wrong but cannot be confidently emended. In this translation Wellesley's suggestion *non in poenam certaturi* has been adopted.

Chapter 33, 'by loyal service – yours and my own': Some editors, following the first printed edition, alter the manuscript reading *opera nostra* to *opera vestra*. But the change is unnecessary. All through the passage Agricola is talking in balanced phrases both of his soldiers and of himself; *nostra* is thus equivalent to *mea et vestra*, 'our combined' (OR).

'When will they come and fight us?': Reading *quando in manus venient?* for the meaningless *quando animus* of the Jesi manuscript.

Chapter 34, 'in the night': See Chapter 26 for this nocturnal attack.

'fifty years': A round figure, and well off the mark: the time is actually forty-two years (A.D. 43–84).

Chapter 35, 'vastly more glorious': A curious phrase to apply to the wise and economical policy of sparing the legionaries, whose recruitment and training were expensive, and using instead the auxiliaries, who were cheaper and easier to get.

Chapter 38, 'Trucculensis Portus': Neither the name nor the position of this harbour is known. If it was somewhere on the Firth of Tay or the Firth of Forth, the fleet apparently sailed up the east coast and along the north coast, and probably turned back after doubling Cape Wrath. The voyage is the one referred to in Chapter 10.

Chapter 39, 'his sham triumph over Germany': Domitian triumphed over the Chatti in A.D. 83. Frontinus records a genuine victory, and modern archaeology has confirmed his account. Tacitus is repeating malicious gossip, which Domitian asked for by making a fool of himself in connection with this triumph.

'the monopoly of the emperor': The emperor was 'imperator' *par excellence*; hence the word 'emperor'. When first proclaimed emperor he assumed the title *imp(erator)*, and often used it, as a sort of praenomen, at the head of his official title. Any important victory won by one of his legates might earn for the emperor a fresh salutation as *imperator*. These salutations were recorded by the abbreviation *imp.*, with a numeral, at the end of his title.

Chapter 40, 'in the Senate': The emperor's decisions were often made effective by *senatus consulta*, decrees of the Senate proposed by him and duly ratified by the obedient senators.

Chapter 41, 'armies were lost': The fighting referred to went on from A.D. 85 to *c.* 93. The chief enemies were the Daci, the Quadi, and the Sarmatian Iazyges. One of the worst disasters was the loss of the praetorian prefect Cornelius Fuscus, with nearly all his army, in the Dobrudja in 86.

'the general slackness': Reading *aliorum* for *eorum*, the difficult reading of the manuscripts (retained in OR).

Chapter 42, 'Africa or Asia': These provinces, governed by pro-consuls, were two of the crowning prizes of a senatorial career. Normally the lot decided between the two senior ex-consuls who had not yet held either post. The date must have been A.D. 90 or a little later. C. Vettulenus Civica Cerialis was executed while governor of Asia in 88/9.

'not wishing ... to accept': Tacitus's usually acute sense of logic deserted him for a moment when he wrote *ne quod vetuerat videretur emisse* – literally 'lest he might appear to have bought what he had in fact forbidden'. This does not really make sense – though few editors seem to have noticed the fact. There are two possible lines of explanation: *quod vetuerat emisse* may be taken to mean either (1) 'to have used bribery in a matter in which he had in fact issued a prohibition'; or (2) 'to have bought Agricola's acquiescence in his prohibition' – assuming that Tacitus, in his passion for brevity, has omitted an essential idea.

Chapter 43, 'a persistent rumour': Tacitus admits that there was no good evidence for the truth of the rumour, but perhaps hoped his readers would believe it (OR).

'named Domitian as co-heir': It was a common practice to bequeath a part of one's estate to the emperor in order to secure the remainder for one's family. Naturally, the practice flourished in inverse proportion to the virtue of the reigning emperor. But good emperors also received legacies. The character of Domitian was in some ways so bad that as soon as he was dead he became an easy target for attack. But in this chapter Tacitus is less than fair to him.

Chapter 44, 'Agricola was born ... Priscinus': Agricola was born in A.D. 40 and died in 93. The manuscript readings *sexto* and *Prisco* need to be corrected into *quarto* and *Priscino*.

'the principate of Trajan': Trajan distinguished himself in A.D. 89 by helping to suppress the revolt of Antonius Saturninus. Adopted by Nerva in the autumn of 97, he succeeded him on his death in January, 98. That his advancement should have been hopefully prophesied is quite credible, though not recorded elsewhere.

Chapter 45, 'Agricola did not live to see': The reign of terror began about the time of his death. Among the noble ladies exiled were

Arria, widow of Thrasea Paetus, and her daughter Fannia, wife of Helvidius Priscus. Domitian's informers were let loose; victims were brought to trial before the Senate and sentenced to exile or death.

'watched in shame . . . innocent blood': The manuscripts have *nos Maurici Rusticique visus, nos innocenti sanguine Senecio perfudit*. It is very difficult to take *visus* ('sight'), as well as *Senecio*, as a subject of *perfudit*. Editors assume that a verb (e.g. *foedavit* or *adflixit*) has dropped out after *visus*.

'blood-red countenance': Domitian was of a rubicund complexion, which made it impossible for him to *turn* red with shame.

'long absence': Tacitus was absent from Rome holding some provincial appointment from A.D. 89 or 90 to 93. It is characteristic of him that he omits to tell us what the appointment was.

'some tears . . . were not shed': This translation follows most of the manuscripts and most editors in reading *comploratus es*. OR adopt the variant reading *compositus es*, 'you were laid out for burial'.

Chapter 46, 'With many . . . fame': The extant manuscripts have *multos veterum velut inglorios et ignobilis oblivio obruet*. Although this text is defended by OR, it seems strange for Tacitus to prophesy that many men of early times, although still (presumably) remembered today, will be forgotten in the future. This translation follows the reading which a fifteenth century scholar says he found in the Jesi manuscript (then in a more complete state than it is now): *multos veluti inglorios et ignobiles oblivio obruet*. If *veterum* is omitted as an interpolation, the future tense *obruet* is quite natural. If *veterum* is retained, the conjecture *obruit* (perfect) seems necessary.

NOTES ON THE GERMANIA

All the extant manuscripts of the *Germania* (nearly thirty in number) date from the 15th or early 16th century, and are believed to have been derived ultimately from a single archetype of the 9th century.

The text followed in this translation is in the main that of Anderson (Oxford Press, 1938). Notes refer to some passages where a special textual difficulty calls for comment.

Chapter 1, 'a campaign of the present century': The campaign referred to is assumed to be that of Tiberius in A.D. 5, which was conducted by land and sea; *nuper*, 'recently', seems to be used rather loosely, but this can be paralleled.

Chapter 2, 'defies intruders': Some people take *adversus* to mean 'antipodal', although Tacitus elsewhere betrays his ignorance of the spherical shape of the earth. But the sense 'hostile' seems more appropriate. The emendation *aversus*, 'turning its back', is not necessary.

'from our part of the world': 'Our' of course means 'Roman', as often; thus *mare nostrum* is the Mediterranean.

'to frighten them': The Tungri told the Gauls that across the Rhine there were vast numbers of their kinsmen – *Germani* like themselves – who would be ready to reinforce them in case of need.

Chapter 3, Footnote: This digression on the German war-chant comes rather awkwardly in the main body of the text. Although *barditum* has better manuscript authority than *baritum*, the correct form of the word is almost certainly *baritus* or *barritus*; it means 'roar' – of an elephant for example.

Chapter 4, 'remain of pure blood': The claim to special purity of race had been made before Tacitus's time for various other peoples. He can never have dreamed of the terrible abuses which would grow out of his simple statement.

Chapter 5, 'it will not grow fruit-trees': Tacitus is probably thinking especially of the most important fruit-trees of Mediterranean countries – the vine and the olive.

'Silver and gold have been denied them': Finds of precious metals in Germany are numerous enough to show that we must not take Tacitus too seriously here.

'old-fashioned coins': The *pecunia vetus* was the denarius of the Republic. The *serrati* had notches in their edges, intended to show that the metal was solid; *bigati* had as reverse type Diana or Victory in a two-horse chariot (*biga*). These two classes of coins seem to be used, with some inaccuracy, to denote the earlier Roman silver coinage in general.

Chapter 6, 'the sort of weapons they have': Tacitus's account of German arms is often corroborated by the evidence of coins, statuettes, and reliefs.

'The Hundred': Tacitus's *centeni* have nothing to do with the 'hundreds' into which many Germanic states were divided at a much later date. Some scholars think that the designation *centeni* – 'a title of distinction', as he calls it – must have belonged to the horsemen rather than to the select infantrymen who accompanied them in battle. But his statement cannot be disproved; it may well be that he was really speaking for the moment of an infantry *élite*.

Chapter 8, 'turning women into goddesses': The last sentence of this chapter is clearly intended as a severe criticism of the Roman practice of deifying women. Drusilla, sister of the emperor Gaius, Claudia Augusta the infant daughter of Nero and Poppaea, and Poppaea herself, had been consecrated as goddesses (*Divae*). Tacitus seems to have accepted the consecration of men as a political necessity: he normally gives the title *Divus* to emperors who had been consecrated.

Chapter 9, 'Mercury . . . Hercules and Mars': Mercury represents the German Wodan, whose name is preserved in Wednesday; Hercules, Donar (Norse Thor: Thursday); Mars, Tiu (Tuesday).

'Some of the Suebi sacrifice also to Isis': Tacitus thinks that the goddess worshipped was the Egyptian Isis, not a German goddess identified with her. The galley suggests advent by sea; Isis was worshipped in many places as the protectress of ships, and a spring festival, 'the release of ships', was celebrated in her honour when the winter storms were past.

Chapter 11, 'the chiefs': There is no difficulty about *principes*, if we remember that they were simply nobles – men prominent by wealth or birth – not magistrates, though capable of being chosen for magisterial posts.

Chapter 12, 'are pressed down . . . a bog': Matthew Arnold's lines (in *Balder Dead*, Part 2) come to mind:

> Cowards, who were in sloughs interr'd alive;
> And round them still the wattled hurdles hung,
> Wherewith they stamp'd them down, and trod them deep,
> To hide their shameful memory from men.

Over fifty victims of this punishment have been found in north-western Europe.

'a hundred assessors': The *centeni* occur again here in a new context, and again the objections raised against Tacitus's account are inconclusive.

Chapter 13, 'the rank of "chief"': Tacitus can hardly mean that these youths immediately assumed the position of fully-fledged chiefs. Clearly they did not at once take a prominent position, but were attached as followers to those who were older and more experienced. They were *principes*, as Anderson says, 'in the same anticipatory sense as a child of the house is *dominus*' (see Chapter 20).

Chapter 17: Tacitus's account of German dress is generally proved correct where details can be checked by ancient reliefs or coins.

Chapter 20, 'childlessness': The childless old man or woman (*orbus*, *orba*) and their courtiers (*captatores*), who were after their money, were a joke and a scandal at Rome in the early Empire. Calvia Crispinilla, for example, a disreputable old noblewoman at Nero's court, survived his fall and lived unscathed through the troubled reigns of Galba, Otho, and Vitellius, enjoying great influence from her wealth and childlessness (Tacitus, *Histories* I, 73).

Chapter 21, *ad finem*: The words *victus inter hospites comis* are bracketed as an interpolation by Anderson, following most other editors.

Chapter 24, 'one kind of public show': This is the famous sword dance (originally, spear dance), not unknown even today.

Chapter 25: This account of slavery in Germany is scanty and in some ways inaccurate.

'Freedmen rank little higher than slaves': Tacitus seems to take a rather malicious pleasure in emphasizing the powerlessness of freedmen in Germany. At Rome, freedmen sometimes made large fortunes by daring speculation. In the service of Claudius and his successors they came to have considerable political influence, especially as the heads of important administrative bureaux – Finance, Correspondence, etc. Tacitus's *bête noire* Domitian had his confidential freedmen.

Chapter 29, '*agri decumates*': These lands, situated between the Rhine, Main, and Danube, were included in the empire by Vespasian and his successors. The name *decumates* is pre-Roman and does not mean 'tithe-lands'; perhaps 'lands of ten cantons'.

Chapter 31: Tacitus speaks as if he did not realize the distinction between the young men who are still unshorn because they have not killed their man; the non-military types who must perforce remain unshorn all their lives; and the 'many' who retain or resume the habit because they like it. By letting their hair and beard grow long even in peace time, they are ready to terrify enemies by their appearance when war starts again. These last were probably a special caste of dedicated warriors.

Chapter 33, 'The Bructeri were defeated': Probably in A.D. 98. The men of the Roman army of Lower Germany were apparently watching the battle, which to them was like a great gladiatorial show. The tribe was not so completely destroyed as Tacitus says. Perhaps as a sequel to this war, a Roman general, Vestricius Spurinna, placed a king of the Bructeri on the throne.

'destiny is driving our empire': The words *urgentibus imperii fatis* seem to mean the same as *urgentibus imperium fatis* would mean: 'now that the fates of the empire are driving it on'. The tone is certainly anxious, perhaps even pessimistic, about the future of the empire. The strain is growing too great, the burden too heavy. If Tacitus does not despair, it is because fate has still one precious gift to help Rome – dissension among her foes.

Chapter 34, 'Drusus Germanicus': This is Nero Claudius Drusus (brother of the emperor Tiberius), who campaigned in Germany in 12–9 B.C. and died there in the latter year. He is said to have been the first Roman to explore the northern seas.

'Since then no one has attempted it': This apparently means that no one has since attempted to inquire into the secrets of Hercules. For voyages in the north were undertaken both by Tiberius in A.D. 5 and by Germanicus in 15–16.

Chapter 35, 'the Chauci': Received into alliance by Drusus in 12 B.C. In A.D. 28 they joined in the Frisian revolt, and they fought for Civilis in 69–70. Tacitus's high praise is not fully borne out by other authorities. Part of them lived in poverty on the coast and tried to improve their condition by piracy, which led them into trouble with Rome in 41 and 47.

Chapter 36, 'the Cherusci': Arminius, the famous chief of this tribe, died in A.D. 21. It received a king from the Romans in 47. Its king Chariomerus, driven out by the Chatti *c.* 85, obtained financial help, but nothing more, from Domitian.

Chapter 37, 'in her six hundred and fortieth year': The date is 113 B.C.

'the second consulship of the emperor Trajan': A.D. 98.

'Such is the time it is taking to conquer Germany': Compare the last sentence of this chapter: 'the more recent "victories" claimed by our commanders have been little more than excuses for celebrating triumphs'. The Romans were not accustomed to the kind of resistance that the Germans put up against them. For an account of the various German wars, see Introduction, Section X.

'the Samnites': Contested with Rome the control of central Italy in three wars, lasting from 343 to 290 B.C. The bitterest blow to Rome was the defeat and capitulation of her army at the Caudine Forks in 321.

'the Carthaginians': Also fought three wars against Rome – the first Punic war, 264–241 B.C.; the second (the great war with Hannibal), 218–201; the third, ending in the destruction of Carthage, 149–146. In the first war Rome lost a consular army under Regulus in Africa and more than one fleet in storms at sea. In the second war Hannibal routed great Roman armies at the river Trebia, lake Trasimene, and Cannae, marched up and down Italy at will for ten years, and at one moment threatened the very existence of Rome.

'Spain': The conquest of Spain began in the second Punic war and was only rounded off under Augustus. The Lusitanians under Viriathus (c. 150–139 B.C.) and the Celtiberians of Numantia (c. 141–133) inflicted serious losses on the Romans.

'Gaul': In 390 B.C. Gauls invaded Italy, defeated the Romans at the river Allia, and sacked Rome. For over a century and a half they continued to cause much trouble on the northern frontier.

'the Parthians': M. Crassus the triumvir invaded Parthia, without just reason, but was defeated and killed at Carrhae in Mesopotamia in 53 B.C., with very heavy loss. Later, the Parthians took the offensive under Pacorus, son of their king Orodes. But he in his turn was defeated and killed at the fortress of Gindarus in Syria (38) by P. Ventidius, an able but allegedly low-born legate of Mark Antony.

Chapter 38, 'tie it in a knot': The knots of the Suebi are well illustrated on various monuments.

Chapter 39, 'The districts . . . number a hundred': This seems a large number of districts for a single tribe. Perhaps it includes the other tribes that shared in the festival.

Chapter 41, 'the splendid colony': This can be none other than Augusta Vindelicorum (Augsburg). But *colonia* is a misnomer.

When the *Germania* was written it was just a town (*civitas*), but was raised by Hadrian to the status of a *municipium*.

'a river well-known': Two or three Roman expeditions had reached the Elbe; but a plan to make it a frontier of the empire was abandoned after the defeat of Varus in A.D. 9.

Chapter 42, 'Tudrus': Since Maroboduus was certainly a great king of the Marcomanni, Tudrus must have been a king of the Quadi. But he is known only from this passage.

Chapter 43, 'inasmuch as they work iron mines': The reason why the Cotini ought to be ashamed is because they could use the iron to make weapons and win their freedom, instead of tamely paying tribute.

'Castor and Pollux': The deities of the Naharvali are two in number, young men, and brothers, their native name being 'Alci'. By *interpretatio Romana* Tacitus means the identification of foreign deities with those deities in the Graeco-Roman pantheon to whom they correspond most nearly. In this case Castor and Pollux – the Greek Dioscuri, heavenly twins, saviours on land and sea – are the obvious choice.

Chapter 45, 'Popular belief adds': The sun-god was commonly represented in ancient art as a charioteer with a crown of rays on his head, driving a horse-drawn chariot.

'amber': This material was used for decoration from very early times, and some was imported into Italy from the early Republican period onwards. In the second century A.D. there was a flourishing trade in it between Italy and the shore of the Baltic.

Chapter 46, 'the repulsive appearance of the Sarmatians': Referring to the wide nostrils and slanting eyes of some Asiatic peoples.

SELECT BIBLIOGRAPHY

THE AGRICOLA AND THE GERMANIA
Text
H. Furneaux, *Taciti Opera Minora*, Oxford Classical Texts, 1900.
Edition
J. H. Sleeman, *Agricola and Germania*, Cambridge, 1914; 7th edition, 1958.
Translations
A. J. Church and W. J. Brodribb, London, 2nd edition, 1877.
M. Hutton, Loeb Classical Library, 1914; 8th edition, 1963.

AGRICOLA
Editions
J. G. C. Anderson, Oxford, 1922; a revision of Furneaux's edition of 1898.
E. de Saint-Denis, *Tacite: Vie d'Agricola*, Paris, 3rd edition, 1956.
R. M. Ogilvie and I. A. Richmond, Oxford, 1967; a revision of the Furneaux-Anderson edition, with important new material.

GERMANIA
Editions
R. P. Robinson, *The Germania of Tacitus*, Middletown, 1935.
J. G. C. Anderson, Oxford, 1938.
J. Perret, *La Germanie*, Paris, 1949; Budé edition with French translation and notes.
G. Forni and F. Galli, Rome, 1964; Italian notes and a comprehensive bibliography.
Character and Sources
E. Norden, *Die germanische Urgeschichte in Tacitus' Germania*, Berlin-Leipzig, 1920; 4th edition, 1959.

SELECT BIBLIOGRAPHY

GENERAL

R. Syme, *Tacitus*, Oxford, 1958, 2 volumes; see especially Chapter XI.

Cambridge Ancient History, Vol. XI (1936), Chapter XI: *Flavian Wars and Frontiers*, by R. Syme.

ROMAN BRITAIN

A selection of recent books:

E. Birley, *Roman Britain and the Roman Army*, 2nd edition, 1961.

A. R. Burn, *Agricola and Roman Britain*, London, 1953.

S. S. Frere, *Britannia, a History of Roman Britain*, London, 1967.

I. A. Richmond, *Roman Britain*, London, 2nd edition, 1963 (Pelican Book).

A. L. F. Rivet, *Town and Country in Roman Britain*, 2nd edition, 1964.

Ordnance Survey, Map of Roman Britain, 3rd edition.

GLOSSARY OF PERSONS, PLACES, AND CERTAIN SUBJECTS

References are to sections of the Introduction and to chapters o, Agricola and Germania.

ABNOBA. G. 1. The Black Forest.

AEDILE. I. xii.

AEMILIUS SCAURUS, M. A. 1. Consul 115 and 107 B.C.

AESTII. G. 45. On east coast of Baltic, in Esthonia.

AFRICA. I. xiii; A. 42; G. 2. Senatorial province, 146 B.C.

AGRICOLA. *See* JULIUS.

AGRIPPINENSES. G. 28. The people of Cologne (Colonia), founded by Claudius in A.D. 50, with the name of his wife, Agrippina II.

ALA. I. xiv; A. 37. Squadron of cavalry.

ALBAN CITADEL. A. 45. The villa of Domitian on the Alban Mount, the scene of his secret councils.

ALBIS. I. ix; G. 41. The Elbe. Augustus gave up the attempt to advance his frontier to it after the destruction of Varus in A.D. 9.

ALBRINIA (or ALBRUNA). *See* AURINIA.

ALCI. G. 43. Brother gods, like Castor and Pollux, worshipped by the Naharvali.

ALPS, RAETIAN. G. 1. Mount St. Gotthard.

AMBER. G. 45.

ANGLII. G. 40. In Schleswig; ancestors of the Angles.

ANGRIVARII. G. 33, 34. On both banks of the middle Weser.

ANTONINUS PIUS. I. vii. Emperor A.D. 138–161.

AQUITANIA. A. 9. Imperial province in S. Gaul, *c.* 27 B.C.

ARAVISCI. G. 28. In north-east Hungary.

ARCADES. A. 21. Centres of shopping and gossip.

ARIOVISTUS. I. x.

ARISTOTLE. I. ix. Great Greek philosopher and writer, 384–322 B.C.

ARMINIUS. I. x. Hermann, chief of the Cherusci, victor over Varus in A.D. 9.

ARMS. I. ix; G. 6, 13.

ARMY. I. viii, xiii, xiv.

ARSACES. G. 37. Legendary founder of the Parthian kingdom, 248 B.C. The name was regularly borne by later Parthian kings.

ARULENUS RUSTICUS, Q. JUNIUS. A. 2, 45. Sentenced to death in A.D. 93 for his eulogy of Thrasea Paetus.

AS. I. xiv. Roman copper coin.

ASCIBURGIUM. G. 3. Near Asberg on lower Rhine.

ASIA. I. i, xiii; A. 6, 42; G. 2. Senatorial province, 133 B.C.

ATILIUS RUFUS. A. 40.

ATTICUS, AULUS. A. 37.

AUGUSTUS. I. i, v, x, xi, xiii, xiv; A. 13. First Roman emperor, 27 B.C.–A.D. 14. *See also* CAESAR.

AURELIUS SCAURUS, M. G. 37. Legate of Mallius Maximus, and with him routed by the Cimbri and Teutoni at Arausio (Orange), 105 B.C.

AURINIA. G. 8.

AUSPICES. G. 10.

AUXILIA. I. xiv; A. 35.

AVIONES. G. 40. In north Frisian islands.

BAEBIUS. *See* MASSA.

BANQUETS. I. ix; A. 21; G. 22.

A luxurious vice of the Empire.

BARITUS (or BARDITUS). G. 3. German war-chant.

BASTARNAE. G. 46. Along line of Carpathians, from Galicia southwards.

BATAVI. I. viii; A. 36; G. 29. On Rhine island, between Rhine and Waal.

BATHS. A. 21. A luxurious vice of the Empire.

BIGATI. G. 5. Denarii of the Roman Republic, with a two-horse chariot (*biga*) on the reverse.

BODOTRIA. I. vii; A. 23, 25. The Forth.

BOIHAEMIUM, BOII. I. x; G. 28, 42. Bohemia. The Boii were expelled from it in 8 B.C. by the Marcomanni.

BORESTI. A. 38. Unknown tribe of the Highlands.

BOUDICCA. I. v, xi; A. 16, 31. Queen of the Iceni in East Anglia. Led revolt against Rome in A.D. 61. Means 'Victory'. 'Boadicea' is an incorrect modern form.

BRIGANTES. I. v; A. 17, 31. Large tribe occupying nearly all the north of England.

BRITAIN (BRITANNIA, BRITANNI).

I. iv ff.; A. *passim;* G. 45.
Imperial province, A.D. 43.

BRUCTERI. I. x; G. 33. Near
Münster

BURI. G. 43. In Moravia.

CAECILIUS METELLUS. G. 37.
Consul 113 B.C.

CAEPIO. *See* SERVILIUS.

CAESAR (=Emperor). I. xii;
A. 4.

CAESAR (=Prince). I. xii.

CAESAR (=Augustus). G. 37.

CAESAR. *See* JULIUS and under
names of emperors.

CAESAR, C. (CALIGULA). I. v,
x, xi; A. 4, 13, 44; G. 37.
Emperor A.D. 37–41.

CALEDONIA. I. vi; A. 10, 11,
25 ff., 31. The Highlands.

CALGACUS. A. 29 ff.

CALIGULA. *See* CAESAR, C.

CAMULODUNUM (Colchester).
I. v; A. 14, 16, 31.

CARATACUS (CARACTACUS).
I. v.

CARBO. *See* PAPIRIUS.

CARUS METTIUS. A. 45. A hated
informer under Domitian.

CASSIUS LONGINUS, L. G. 37.
Consul 107 B.C., defeated by
the Tigurini, allies of the
Cimbri.

CASTOR. G. 43. He and Pollux,

the Heavenly Twins, were
'Saviour Gods' by land and
sea.

CAVALRY. I. xiv; A. 35 ff.; G. 6,
32.

CENTURION. I. xiv; A. 15, 19,
22, 28.

CENTURY. I. xiv.

CEREALIS. *See* PETILIUS.

CHAMAVI. G. 33, 34. Moved by
Nero Drusus into Oberyssel
in Holland.

CHARIOTEERS. A. 35, 36.

CHASUARII. G. 34. North of
Osnabrück.

CHATTI. I. x, xi; G. 29, 30–32,
35, 36, 38. In Hesse. Domitian
waged war on them in A.D. 83
and 89.

CHAUCI. G. 35, 36. From lower
Ems to Elbe.

CHERUSCI. I. x; G. 36. On
middle Weser. Their chief,
Arminius, destroyed Varus
his legions in A.D. 9.

CHIEFS. I. ix; G. 11–15, 22.

CICERO, M. TULLIUS. I. i. Great
Roman orator and writer, 1st
century B.C.

CIMBRI. I. x; G. 37. In Jutland.
Migrated with Teutoni in
113 B.C., won many victories
over Roman armies, harried
Gaul and Spain; finally

ISIS. G. 9. The famous mother-goddess of Egypt.

ISOCRATES. I. iii. Greek orator and essayist, 4th century B.C.

ISTAEVONES. G. 2.

ITALIA. G. 2, 37. Italy.

JULIA PROCILLA. A. 4. Mother of Agricola.

JULIUS AGRICOLA, CN. I. ii, iv, vi; A. *passim.*

JULIUS, DIVUS. I. ii–v, ix–xi; A. 13, 15; G. 28, 37. Name of Julius Caesar, the Dictator, after death and consecration.

JULIUS FRONTINUS, SEX. I. v, vi; A. 17. Governor of Britain, A.D. 74–78. Wrote on Aqueducts and on Stratagems.

JULIUS GRAECINUS. A. 4. Father of Agricola.

JUNIUS MAURICUS RUSTICUS. A. 45. Exiled by Domitian.

KINGS. A. 12–15; G. 7, 10, 11, 12, 43, 44.

KNIGHTS. I. xii, xiv; A. 4.

LAERTES. G. 3.

LANGOBARDI. G. 40. The Lombards. In north-east Hanover.

LAUREL-WREATHED DISPATCHES. A. 18. Used to announce victories.

LAW, ADMINISTRATION OF. A. 6.

LEGATUS CONSULARIS. I. xiv; A. 7.

LEGATUS LEGIONIS. I. xiv; A. 7.

LEGATUS PRAETORIUS. I. xiv; A. 7.

LEGATUS PROVINCIAE. I. xiii; A. 14 ff.

LEGIO II ADIUTRIX. I. viii.

LEGIO II AUGUSTA. I. viii.

LEGIO IX HISPANA. I. viii; A. 26, 34.

LEGIO XIV GEMINA. I. viii.

LEGIO XX VALERIA. I. viii; A. 7.

LEGIONS. I. viii, xiv; A. 35.

LEMOVII. G. 43. In north-east Germany.

LEVY. A. 7, 13, 15, 31.

LIBURNICA. I. xiv; A. 28. A swift, light warship.

LICINIUS CRASSUS, M. G. 37. Defeated and killed by Parthians at Carrhae, 53 B.C.

LIGURIA. A. 7.

LIVIUS, T. I. ix; A. 10. Livy, great Roman historian of the age of Augustus.

LOTS. G. 10.

LUGII (LYGII). G. 43. A large group of south-eastern Germans.

MALLIUS MAXIMUS, CN. G. 37. Consul 105 B.C.; defeated in

that year by Cimbri at Orange (Arausio).

MANIMI. G. 43. In south-east Germany.

MANIPLE. I. xiv; A. 28.

MANNUS. G. 2.

MARCOMANNI. I. x; G. 42, 43. In Bohemia.

MARCUS AURELIUS. I. x. Emperor A.D. 161–180.

MARIUS, C. I. x; G. 37. Defeated Teutoni at Aix-en-Provence (Aquae Sextiae) in 102 B.C., and, with Catulus, defeated Cimbri at Vercellae in 101 B.C.

MAROBODUUS. I. x; G. 42.

MARRIAGE, GODS OF. G. 18.

MARS. G. 9. Roman god of war, the German Tiu.

MARSI. G. 2.

MARSIGNI. G. 43. North or north-east of Bohemia.

MASSA BAEBIUS. A. 45. Notorious informer under Domitian. On trial in A.D. 93 for abuses committed as governor of Baetica.

MASSILIA. A. 4. Marseilles. Founded by Greeks in the 7th century B.C.

MATER DEUM. G. 45. German goddess, Nerthus or Freyja; the Roman Cybele.

MATTIACI. G. 29. On Rhine and Main. 'Aquae Mattiacae', the modern Wiesbaden.

MAURICUS RUSTICUS. See JUNIUS.

MAXIMUS. See MALLIUS.

MERCURIUS. G. 9. Identified with the German Wodan.

MESSALINUS, L. VALERIUS CATULLUS. A. 45. Blind informer under Domitian.

METALS, PRECIOUS. I. ix; G. 5.

METELLUS. See CAECILIUS.

METTIUS. See CARUS.

MINES. A. 31, 32.

MOENUS. G. 28. The Main.

MOESIA. A. 41. On the lower Danube. Imperial province, c. A.D. 6; later, two provinces, Upper and Lower, c. A.D. 86.

MONA. I. v; A. 14, 18. Anglesey.

MONEY. G. 5.

MUCIANUS, C. LICINIUS. A. 7. Governor of Syria A.D. 67–69; chief supporter of Vespasian in his bid for empire.

NAHARVALI (or NAHANARVALI). G. 43. In Silesia.

NAMES. A Roman commonly had three names: (1) a

praenomen, personal name –
L. = Lucius, Sex. = Sextus,
etc.; (2) a *nomen*, name of his
clan (*gens*) – *e.g.* Flavius,
Iulius; (3) a *cognomen*, name
of his family – *e.g.* Caesar,
Scaurus. An extra name
(*agnomen*) was sometimes
added: it might refer to a
personal characteristic – *e.g.*
Cunctator, 'Delayer'; or to
an honour won – *e.g.*
Germanicus, 'Conqueror of
Germany'.

NARISTI. G. 42. West of the
Bohemian forest.

NEMETES. G. 28. In region of
Speyer.

NERO. I. i, v, xi; A. 6, 45.
Emperor A.D. 54–68.

NERO (= TIBERIUS). G. 37. An
exceptional use.

NERO DRUSUS. I. x; G. 37.
Brother of Tiberius. Fought
in Germany 12–9 B.C. and
died there in the latter year.

NERTHUS. G. 40. Terra Mater
or Mother Earth.

NERVA. I. i, iii, x, xi; A. 3.
Emperor A.D. 96–98. In A.D.
97 adopted Trajan.

NERVA TRAIANUS. *See* TRAIANUS

NERVII. G. 28. Round Bavai
and Cambrai.

NORICUM. G. 5. Styria and
Tyrol. Imperial province
(procuratorial), *c.* 15 B.C.

NUITONES (NUITHONES). G. 40.
On coast of Mecklenburg.

OCCIDENS. A. 30; G. 45. The
West.

OCEANUS. A. 10, 12, 15, 25, 40;
G. 1–3, 17, 34, 37, 40, 43, 44.

ORCADES. I. iv; A. 10. The
Orkneys.

ORDOVICES. A. 18. In central
and north Wales.

ORIENS. A. 30; G. 37, 45. The
East.

ORNAMENTS OF TRIUMPH. A. 40,
44.

OSI. G. 28, 43. Near the river
Eipel, on Danube.

OSTORIUS SCAPULA, P. I. v; A.
14. Governor of Britain A.D.
47–52.

OTHO. I. xi; A. 7. Emperor
A.D. 69.

OXIONES. G. 46. Fabulous
people in north.

PACORUS. G. 37. Son of
Parthian king Orodes; killed
in battle against Ventidius, 38
B.C.

PAETUS. *See* THRASEA.

PALACE. A. 40. On the Palatine
Hill in Rome.

PROCONSUL. I. xiii; A. 6, 42.

PROCURATOR. I. xii, xiii; A. 9, 15.

PROPRAETOR. I. xiii.

PROVINCES. I. xii–xiv.

PUBLICANUS. G. 29.
Tax-gatherer.

PYTHEAS. I. iv. Of Massilia,
traveller and writer, late 3rd
century B.C.

QUADI. I. x; G. 42, 43. In
Moravia.

QUAESTOR. I. xii, xiii; A. 6.

QUINCTILIUS VARUS, P. I. x;
G. 37. Destroyed with three
legions by Arminius in A.D. 9.

RAETIA. G. 1, 3, 41. East
Switzerland. Imperial
province (procuratorial), c.
15 B.C.

RELIGION. I. xii; G. 7–9, 39, 40,
43, 45.

REUDIGNI. G. 40. In Holstein.

RHAETIA. See RAETIA.

RHENUS. I. x; G. 1–3, 28, 29, 32,
34, 41, 45. The Rhine.

ROMANI. A. passim. G. 28, 30,
34, 41, 43.

RUFUS. See ATILIUS.

RUGII. G. 43. On west of
Vistula in Pomerania.

RUSTICUS. See ARULENUS and
FABIUS.

RUTILIUS RUFUS, P. A. 1.
Consul 105 B.C.; unjustly
condemned in 92 B.C. for
extortion in Asia, he retired
into residence there.

SALARY OF PROCONSUL. A. 42.

SALLUST. I. i, iii. Roman
historian, 1st century B.C.

SALVIUS TITIANUS. A. 6.
Proconsul of Asia A.D. 63–
64; brother of Otho,
emperor A.D. 69.

SAMNITES. G. 37. The Samnites
fought bitter wars against
Rome, c. 343–290 B.C.

SARMATIA. I. x, xi; G. 1, 17, 43,
46. North of Danube.

SCAPULA. See OSTORIUS.

SCAURUS. See AEMILIUS and
AURELIUS.

SCOUTS. A. 26, 38.

SEMNONES. G. 39. Between
middle Elbe and Oder.

SENATE. I. i, xi–xiv; A. 4, 40, 45.

SENECIO. See HERENNIUS.

SEPTIMIUS SEVERUS. I. vii.
Emperor A.D. 193–211

SERRATI, G. 5. Republican
denarii with notched edge.

SERVILIUS CAEPIO, Q. G. 37.
Consul 106 B.C., defeated by
Cimbri at Orange (Arausio)
in 105 B.C.

SHOWS. G. 19, 24.

SILANUS, M. A. 4. Father of first wife of Gaius Caesar; put to death by him in A.D. 38.

SILURES. I. v; A. 11, 17. In South Wales and Monmouthshire.

SITONES. G. 45. Perhaps in Finland.

SLAVES. I. ix; A. 15, 19, 31; G. 20, 24, 25, 38, 40, 45.

SOL. G. 45. The Sun-God.

SQUADRON OF CAVALRY. I. xiv; A. 18, 37.

STRABO. I. iv, ix. Greek writer on geography, late 1st century B.C.

SUARINES. G. 40. On coast of Mecklenburg (?).

SUCCESSION. I. xii.

SUEBI. I. x; A. 28; G. 2, 9, 38, 39, 41, 43, 45, 46. Generic name for Germans of north and east.

SUETONIUS. I. iii. Roman writer of biography, 1st to 2nd century A.D.

SUETONIUS PAULINUS, C. I. v; A. 5, 14, 16, 18. Governor of Britain A.D. 58/59–61.

SUIONES. G. 44, 45. On Baltic.

SYRIA (SURIA). A. 40. Imperial province, 27 B.C. (first established, senatorial, 64 B.C.).

TACITUS. I. i ff.; A. 9, 45.

TAUS. A. 22. The Tay.

TAXES. I. xiii.

TENCTERI. G. 32, 33, 38. On middle Rhine, east of the Usipi.

TERRA MATER. G. 40. Mother Earth. Also called Nerthus.

TEUTOBURGIENSIS SALTUS. I. x.

TEUTONI. I. x.

THRASEA PAETUS, P. A. 2. Famous Stoic driven by Nero to suicide in A.D. 66.

THULE. A. 10. The Shetlands.

TIBERIUS. I. x, xi, xiv; A. 13. Emperor A.D. 14–37. See also NERO.

TITIANUS. See SALVIUS.

TITUS. I. xi. Emperor A.D. 79–81.

TOGA. A. 21. The national Roman wear for men in peace, a thick woollen garment.

TOGATI. A. 9. Wearers of the toga – Roman civilians.

TRAIANUS. I. i, vii, ix, x, xi; A. 3, 44; G. 37. Emperor A.D. 98–117.

TREBELLIUS MAXIMUS, M. I. v; A. 16. Governor of Britain A.D. 63–69.

TREVERI. G. 28. Treves (Trier).

TRIBOCI. G. 28. On Rhine, near Strasbourg.

THE PENGUIN CLASSICS

Some recent and forthcoming volumes

Cicero
MURDER TRIALS
Michael Grant

DEMOSTHENES AND AESCHINES
A. N. W. Saunders

Stendhal
LOVE
Gilbert and Suzanne Sale

Alarcón
THE THREE-CORNERED HAT
M. Alpert

Maupassant
BEL-AMI
Douglas Parmée

Corneille
THE CID/CINNA/THE THEATRICAL ILLUSION
J. Cairncross

BIRDS THROUGH A CEILING OF ALABASTER:
THREE ABBASID POETS
G. B. H. Wightman and A. V. al-Udhari

Livy
ROME AND THE MEDITERRANEAN
Henry Bettenson and A. H. MacDonald

LIVES OF THE LATER CAESARS
Anthony Birley